DUBLIN TODAY

DUBLIN TODAY

PAT LIDDY

The city's changing face in text and illustration, selected from
THE IRISH TIMES

AN IRISH TIMES PUBLICATION

First published December 1984
The Irish Times Limited

Text © Pat Liddy and The Irish Times Limited
Drawings © Pat Liddy
Design Jarlath Hayes
Co-ordination and Distribution by
Irish Times General Services
11-15 D'Olier Street, Dublin 2. Telephone: 792022
Typesetting Printset & Design Ltd., Dublin
Printed in Ireland by Mount Salus Press Ltd., Dublin

ISBN 0 907011 13 6

For my dear wife
Josephine

Contents

Sources

My information was, in the first place, usually gained from interviews with the owners, occupiers or those responsible for the maintainance of each edifice. The knowledge thus gathered was then corroborated and supplemented by an examination of company records, documents, advertising and publicity literature and other available historical manuscripts. For the details of significant events and for the opening of new buildings, I had some recourse to the microfilm backfile of the *The Irish Times*. The *Irish Builder* proved useful in supplying information on architects and builders. The rest came from a store of titbits (cross-checked, of course) accumulated from years of delightful exploration.

Acknowledgements

First, I would like to thank all the people interviewed over the past years for allowing me to examine and use archival material. Their names are too numerous to mention here. There are those who were pestered more than once; Pat Johnston, The Civic Museum; Danny Lynch, The Office of Public Works; Mary Clarke, Archivist Dublin Corporation; David Lawlor, An Post; Frank Fallon, Dublin Corporation; and the City Centre Business Association, for encouragement and support. Special thanks to Tony Farmar, Colm Hanley, Brenda McNiff and Geraldine O'Beirne.

Preface

During the eighteenth century the splendour of Georgian Dublin was second in the British Empire only to London. It was also one of Europe's largest seaports. In the next century the rate of growth slowed down and a certain amount of decay set in. During the Victorian era many fine and sometimes very ambitious new edifices were erected and these combined with all that went before and since have given Dublin its unique streetscapes and skylines.

There have of course been blunders, opportunism and tragedies which have marred this pretty picture. Characterless office and industrial developments, some unfortunate planning decisions, slum clearances, insurrections and the relentless passing of time have taken their deadly toll. But a large amount of our heritage still remains and needs to be cherished.

Here I have taken, for the most part, a fairly broad look at the city as it is today. In order to explore the often undeservedly less well-known buildings and institutions I have had to omit many of their more famous neighbours. However, the result is a wealth of new information gathered for the first time in book form.

Using the contents page as a guide the reader can follow the suggested sequence or adapt it, section by section, to his/her own wishes.

The last twenty years have seen the awakening of an appreciation of our architectural and cultural legacies. Perhaps this book will offer further encouragement in this direction. In any case, if it gives half as much pleasure to the reader as it has given me in assembling it then it will have been worthwhile.

Pat Liddy
December 1984

Introduction

There was a time when Dublin was the everyday experience. You were born there and worked there and went back and forth day after day through its good streets and its mean streets. Even still, if the city is suddenly named, the mind slips a notch and one sees a line of bookstalls and barrows spread along the quays; or shabby men in shabby coats ringing their handbells outside a string of auction rooms. Or trams — dozens of trams — with sparking trolleys weaving slow and intricate patterns about Nelson's Pillar. Or the great front of Harcourt Street Station with the familiar advertisement above it:

> They come as a boon and a blessing to men
> The Pickwick, the Owl and the Waverley pen

That all faded away a long time ago. But when nostalgia draws one back from time to time — as nostalgia always will — the list of absentees grows longer and longer. Where are the Russell Hotel, the Hibernian Hotel, the Winter Palace Gardens? Where are the Guinness barges, the Liffey ferries, the Ballast Office clock? A favourite was that meekest and friendliest of childhood jumbos — Elvery's Elephant. Another sight to bring small feet to a standstill was the soldiers on guard outside the Bank of Ireland with real rifles and a sentry box and a couple of cannons for good measure. Almost opposite was the biggest wonder of all: the enormous Bovril sign high up above College Green, making its free firework display against the night sky. The huge letters lit up to spell out B-O-V-R-I-L, went out, changed colour, lit up again, picked another colour still, then began to mix the colours in criss-cross patterns of inexhaustible variety. All, alas, gone.

Let us be thankful, then, that in the pages that follow, in text and illustration, Pat Liddy has laboured to gather together those riches that are still there to be enjoyed. Most of them one remembers with sufficient affection to seek them out from time to time. Others, unaccountably, had slipped the mind. I had forgotten (well, almost forgotten) the pawnshops and the line of women waiting near Leonard's Corner each Monday morning to pledge the husband's Sunday suit for the umpteenth time. I had also forgotten the Salvation Army bands. On Sundays and on Summer evenings the canal bank at Portobello Bridge was a customary spot where an ensemble of six or eight of them with brass instruments and drum could gather to listen to the preacher and enliven matters at intervals with hymns that sounded like a happy, brassy cheer. And that space of pavement in front of the Dublin Woollen Company: it was the Sunday gathering spot for buskers, jugglers, acrobats and three-card trick men who melted into invisibility if the police chanced along. It is nice to be reminded.

One is grateful, too, for the list of the Liffey's bridges with their new names that are so hard to remember (perhaps one doesn't want to remember). And for the advice to look up from time to time. What has changed at street level may be unaltered above that. You won't see Erin weeping over her stringless Harp above The Irish House on the quays any more, but the Sunlight Chambers in Parliament Street still display those fascinating panels that depict the history and uses of soap (it once belonged to Lever Bros.)

I am glad to be able to boast that I am one of those Dubliners who did not procrastinate so long that the chance to climb the Pillar was lost forever. And at the age of about six I remarked that bullet hole in the ample but apt bosom of Courage on the O'Connell monument. On the other hand, I haven't yet seen the Book of Kells. Perhaps Pat Liddy's dedicated industry will shame me into it.

James Plunkett

O'Connell Street, Dublin's principal artery and one of the world's most renowned boulevards, had a humble and relatively recent genesis. Part of the land of St. Mary's Abbey, it lay outside the main areas of urban growth for many centuries.

It is said the area around Upper O'Connell Street saw some fierce fighting during the famous Battle of Clontarf in 1014 when the Viking occupation forces were badly mauled by the Irish tribal chieftains. This was not the last battle or skirmish to be fought on this site. Destructive and bloody encounters during the 1913 General Strike, the 1916 Rising and the 1922 Civil War took place in the street. The character and face of the thoroughfare abruptly changed after these years. The apparently classier style dates in the main from the 1920s and makes a search for historical connections more difficult than is usual.

Towards the end of the 17th century a narrow street, Drogheda Street, was laid running from present-day Parnell Street to Abbey Street. It was named Drogheda Street after its developer Henry Moore, Earl of Drogheda; Henry Street, Moore Street, Earl Street and even an ''Of'' Lane were all named after him. In the same style, Grafton Street, Duke Street and Harry Street were named after Harry, Duke of Grafton. Drogheda Street was rather dingy and lacked any fine buildings. It petered out into a warren of laneways which gave access to the unbridged river Liffey.

Luke Gardiner, afterwards Lord Mountjoy, acquired the Moore estate and in 1749 commenced a huge development of Drogheda Street. He swept aside every house north of Henry Street and increased the width westwards until an impressive 150 feet was attained. Magnificent town mansions for the rich gentry lined both sides (the only present-day survivor from this period is number 42, the old Catholic Commercial Club) and a mall or walk was placed down the centre. The mall, 50 feet wide and 700 feet long, was marked out with obelisks, a low wall, and a gravelled walk bordered by a double row of elm trees.

A fountain was later added to the northern end. Unrivalled even by the elegance of Bath, it became fashionable for the nobility to promenade for an evening stroll along the street. This upper stretch of Drogheda Street was renamed Sackville Street in 1756 to honour Lionel Sackville, Duke of Dorset and Lord Lieutenant 1731-37 and 1751-55. For many years, however, the street was popularly known as Gardiner's Mall. The Mall was removed in 1791 as was the fountain in 1807. Bartholomew Mosse and his architect Richard Cassels had wanted to close off Sackville Street with the Rotunda Hospital in the 1750s, but were refused permission by Luke Gardiner who wished to continue a northbound expansion.

In 1772 the Wide Street Commissioners made grants available to widen the remainder of Drogheda Street and open access to the river where a bridge was planned. Earlier attempts to do this had failed due to a lack of adequate finance. This work was mostly completed by 1789 and the name changed to Lower Sackville Street. Carlisle Bridge was opened in 1793 and this single act did more than anything to change the central axis of the city and to herald the change of Sackville Street from residential to an office and business centre.

Despite the exodus after the Union the street took on a new importance and significance. Nelson's Pillar was erected in 1808, replacing the earlier statue to General Sir William Blakeney who, at the age of 84, was the hero of the siege of St Phillips Fort in Minorca in 1756. A whole series of statues have followed and these

are dealt with later. The boast of the street, the General Post Office, was opened in 1818. Tramways came to the city when the first horse drawn vehicle left Nelson's Pillar for Rathmines and Terenure on the 1st February, 1872. Old photographs show prosperous looking scenes in Sackville Street with busy footpaths and the wide thoroughfare choked with traffic observing neither lane nor direction discipline. But off the centre stage the storm clouds were gathering. A resolution was passed by Dublin Corporation in 1885 to change the name Sackville Street to O'Connell Street in memory of the Liberator, Daniel O'Connell. Many business people were aghast at the change, feared that they would lose custom, because Sackville Street was known all over Europe. They petitioned the Government, and the Rt. Hon. Hedges Eyre Chatterton, Vice-Chancellor of Ireland, sought and gained an injunction on 19th June restraining the Corporation from making the alteration.

The city officials had to obey the court ruling. Many of the ordinary citizens started using the new name and the Corporation made no attempt to renew the fading name plates on the street's corners.

Huge gathering for political rallies, notable funerals and protest demonstrations became commonplace in Sackville Street during the first decade of the present century. Violence erupted during an address by Jim Larkin to thousands of striking workers in 1913 and a police baton charge resulted in two deaths and hundreds of injuries. Over the next three years various shades of political movements held clandestine meetings in nearby houses and squads of Irish Volunteers openly marched in military order up the street on their way to their assemblies in Rutland (Parnell) Square.

The events of Easter Monday, 24th April, 1916 took everyone by surprise. Most officials were enjoying a day off when around 1,500 insurgents simultaneously occupied many strongpoints in the city. About 60 rebels led by Pearse and Connolly charged into the public office of the G.P.O. and began barricading the place with mail sacks and smashing the front windows. Ironically the office had only reopened a month earlier after a major refurbishment and modernisation.

A week later most of the lower end of Sackville Street and a section from North Earl Street to Cathedral Street was in ruins. The main cause of the fires which raged uncontrolled for days was not the British artillery but the looters who started their frenzied orgy on the first day of the Rising. Sniper fire from the G.P.O. effectively prevented the fire brigade from taking preventive action. In all, 250 building were gutted around the city centre and the human toll was 250 killed and 2,600 wounded. The damage was estimated at £3,000,000; ex-gratia grants were subsequently provided by the Government to start the work of restoration.

The rebuilding programme was first held up by a controversy as to whether facades should be constructed in stone or brick. Then various Bills were enacted imposing re-instatement conditions. A shortage of building materials - the first World War was still raging - also held up reconstruction. The tragic Civil War of 1922 not only caused further delay but resulted in the destruction of most of the east side of Upper O'Connell Street which had escaped damage in 1916. Some of the buildings on the opposite side were also burned down.

With 60% of the street still in rubble in 1923, the nearly bankrupt Free State was confronted with an almost hopeless task. More haggling started as to the architectural styles of the replacement buildings and there was even a suggestion that the long awaited Catholic Cathedral should be erected where the Savoy

cinema now stands. The Criminal and Malicious Injuries (Amendment) Bill insisted that the new buildings "shall be either of the same character as the injured building or of a character suitable to the neighbourhood and not less valuable than the injured building". In 1924 the Corporation was temporarily dissolved and three Commissioners were appointed. Not feeling constrained by the perpetual injunction they formally renamed the street O'Connell Street.

Massed celebrations returned to the thoroughfare in the 1930s. In 1932 hundreds of thousands thronged for a view of the altar on O'Connell Bridge during the Eucharistic Congress. 200,000 attended the Proclamation of the Republic outside the G.P.O. on the 18th April, 1949.

The fortunes of O'Connell Street have since ebbed and flowed.

The Future

Not everyone is enamoured with the way the street has evolved especially since the mid 1960s. But there have been some discernible moves in the last number of years to restore the street to something of its former glory. With a handful of exceptions the fabric is still there to turn O'Connell Street into one of the world's premier boulevards.

The Trees

The greenery in O'Connell Street is provided by 54 trees of varying ages. The 18 mature trees along the centre islands, dating from around the turn of the century, have been recently supplemented by an additional 27 saplings. A further 9 saplings are asserting themselves along the footpaths of the lower end of the street.

The trees themselves are all London planes which are less affected than most other species by pollution. Their roots are able to find nourishment in the marshy sub-soil. In fact the water table is quite high under the street and is even influenced by the tidal actions of the Liffey. Several buildings in the district which are not adequately waterproof at foundation level are often flooded as a result.

The birds which inhabit the trees all year round are pied wagtails who took up residence only about 40 years ago. They were probably encouraged to stay by the snug warmth provided by the Christmas lights in December and January. In the day time they hunt for food in the suburban fields and return to nest in the evening.

The Old Catholic Commercial Club

Designed by Richard Cassels in 1752 the house was remarkable for its fine hallway, palatial rooms, fine staircase and stuccoed ceilings, but today it lies sadly neglected. The Earl of Gosford, from Markethill, Co Armagh, had made it his town residence before handing it over to the trustees of the Royal Agricultural Society in 1861. Two years later it passed to the Irish Farmers' Club.

In 1882, the recently-formed Catholic Commercial Club Company bought the building for conversion to a club for Catholic businessmen who, up to that, had been excluded from the existing social clubs in the city. Their Memorandum of Association named their first objective as: "To promote the moral, social and intellectual improvement of the members, and to provide them with a lending library, reading room, gymnasium, billiards, bagatelle and other amusement rooms, rooms for lectures and a restaurant." Many of Dublin's most famous political, business and artistic sons became associated with the club.

For a while the club remained a bastion of male supremacy. A notice declared: "The stewards and hall porter are instructed that ladies are not to be allowed past the hall, and that in the event of members introducing ladies into the hall, a chair is to be provided and the ladies requested to sit there."

A decade ago the changing trends of business and commercial life forced the club to liquidate its lease on the building. Also lying empty at the rear is the classically-styled O'Connell Hall, famed for its excellent acoustics, and, until recently, the practice hall for the R.T.E. orchestras.

Twice number 42 survived destruction. Once when three shells hit the building in 1916 and again when rebel forces occupied it during the Civil War. It now seems as if only public interest in its history and contribution to city life can save O'Connell Street's last link with the best of its Georgian past.

The block nearest the river on the west side escaped relatively unscathed from the 1916 Rising. The two premises at either end were damaged, including number 56 which, ironically a gunpowder office, was occupied by rebel forces and was later raked by gun and shellfire. This latter building afterwards became noted as the retail outlet for tobacconists Kapp and Peterson Ltd (now Zerep) and although the old firm is gone from here their name is still perpetuated on the four nameplates inset into the mosaic walls at ground level.

The next door building (now Kinahan's Newsagency) is the oldest survivor on this block; the remainder have been substantially altered or rebuilt. Just under the Dutch-style gable is a curious clock which is, in fact, a wind direction dial intended to be operated by the overhead wind vane but which no longer functions. It probably belongs to the time when the clock factory of Chancellor and Son occupied the house.

Number 51 (now two restaurants, the Sunflower and Mandy's) housed the Sackville Picture House for many years. A little further up the road is the modern facade of Burgerland which fits in uncomfortably along this stretch of streetscape. Over the Old Kentucky Restaurant there is a curiosity which stands out from the surrounding facades. Declaring itself to be the Confectioners Hall it dates from the days when Lemons Sweets had a shop and small factory here and was one of the oldest establishments of the kind in Ireland. It was rather grandly described in old advertisements as "Wholesale, Confection, Lozenge and Comfit Manufacturers to the King".

This block has been widely criticised for its honky-tonk image but whatever its visual demerits at ground level the upper stories are varied and interesting and deserve to be better preserved. At least a couple of owners have shown sensitivity in this direction.

Elephant House

Having occupied the corner site for close on 30 years *The Irish Press* put it up for sale in the summer of 1984. Older Dubliners will remember when the premises were the headquarters of Elverys, sports shop and waterproof and gutta percha manufacturers (gutta percha was obtained from the latex of a Malaysian tree and its hard rubber-like quality was used in the making of golf balls etc). In 1916 Elverys had seen an ideal opportunity when they moved from their previous location further down the street to commission their own custom-built emporium on the ruins left after the Rising.

The projecting plinth, used to support a statue of an elephant which had become the symbol of Elverys, gave the name Elephant House to the building. Elverys adopted their trademark from a previous shopkeeper on the same site who was an importer of tea from Ceylon and who also used the elephant motif. The present elephant statue outside Elverys in Suffolk Street is not the original which disintegrated when it was moved from O'Connell Street. Architect, George P. Beater; Contractor, J. and W. Stewart.

Number 43 and 44 was built in 1922 for Manfield and Sons, boot and shoe manufacturers. It replaced their earlier premises which had perished like the rest of this block following the incendiary shelling of the G.P.O. Tylers, another shoe manufacturer, has succeeded Manfields in the ground floor retail outlet. Architect, Batchelor & Hicks, Merrion Square; Steel Works, J. & C. McGloughlin.

The little cul-de-sac illustrated right is situated off Upper Abbey Street (almost opposite Turbetts, Wine Merchants). Its existence often comes as a surprise even when pointed out to regular passers-by. The continued preservation of such housing areas is essential to a balanced city life.

8

PRIV
PARKI

9

Eason & Son Ltd

In 1850 W.H. Smith of London, still a famous name throughout Britain, bought the bankrupt newspaper and advertising agency of J.K. Johnston and Co., Eden Quay. Appointed Chief Secretary for Ireland in 1886 and not wishing to be accused of having a conflict of interests, Smith sold his Irish business to his manager of 30 years, Charles Eason. Ironically, Smith had to vacate his office after only a few months following the collapse of the ruling British Government.

Starting initially with a small bookstall in Sackville Street, the firm rapidly expanded with the growth of the railways and the proliferation of national daily newspapers. At one time 90 bookstalls were located in various railway stations but these have now been whittled down to a small handful. Instead, city centre stores have become the mainstay of the operation which comprises the retailing and wholesaling of books, newspapers, magazines, greeting cards, stationery and goods related to leisure activities. The advertising agency, which can trace its origins back to 1819, is probably the oldest in the country.

The destruction of the shop in Sackville Street in 1916 afforded the opportunity for expansion. Architect, J.A. Ruthven; Builder, P.J. Good Ltd. The present building opened in 1919 and was acclaimed for some interesting innovations. It was one of the first buildings to employ reinforced concrete, and it was so sturdily built that it often defied later attempts at internal modifications. Mirror reflectors were used to enhance the availability of natural light to the 1 ½ acres of floor space.

When the Palm Grove Restaurant was acquired in 1976, Easons went to considerable trouble to match existing entrances of polished Aberdeen red granite. The Easons have been distinguished participants in the life of the city for the last hundred years, and have been associated with many commercial and charitable organisations. Members of the family are still directors of the company.

In the foreground is the statue of Sir John Gray executed by Thomas Farrell and unveiled in 1879.

Adjoining Easons the modern functional facade of the British Home Stores contrasts sharply with the magnificent front of the much-loved Metropole Cinema which it replaced. The Metropole and the neighbouring Capitol Cinema were demolished in 1973. The Metropole Cinema had itself replaced the Metropole Hotel which had an ornate tapestry of wrought iron balconies on each floor.

A contemporary advertisement had boasted that the hotel "had a hundred airy lightsome bedrooms" and was "lighted throughout by electricity and equipped with every scientific appliance to make it safe, comfortable and efficient in its working". It was destroyed in 1916.

P. LIDDY '84

11

The General Post Office

The site chosen for the new General Post Office was earlier made derelict in 1796 with the collapse of three houses in temporary use as a barracks. It had also been suggested that the site would be suitable for the city's proposed Catholic Cathedral. This latter idea was rejected, so soon after Emancipation, when it was feared that the climate was not ripe for placing a church in such a prime position.

The foundation stone of the G.P.O. was laid on the 12th August, 1914 by the Earl of Whitworth, the Lord Lieutenant. The former office in College Green was sold for £11,000 and the new headquarters cost £50,000 to build. It was the first building in Ireland specifically designed as a post office. Granite was used throughout except for the portico, with its six Ionic fluted columns, where Portland stone was used. The style was 18th century Greek Revival. Architectural drawings show that it was the original intention to surmount the building with a high dome, but this plan never came to fruition. Francis Johnston was the architect and his masterpiece was opened to the public on the 6th January, 1818 with 40 staff in attendance.

The 1984 refurbishing of the G.P.O. is a cue to recall the massive undertaking in rebuilding the shattered hulk left in the aftermath of the 1916 Rising. Only the front section, including the portico and the three statues, had somehow escaped relatively unscathed, although you can still see the marks from numerous bullets. Sculpted by Edward Smyth, Hibernia holds spear and harp; Mercury the messenger of the Gods, equipped with canduceus or wand, holds a purse aloft; Fidelity holds a key to her bosom. Rubble choked the gutted and forlorn wreck for three years until a grant of £5,000 was made available by the British Treasury to pay demobbed soldiers to clear the debris. Any further work had to wait until after Independence.

By 1924 the public was clamouring for the work of restoration to commence, and a year later *The Irish Times* could report that: "the Commissioners of Public Works had accepted the tender of Messrs Alex Hull and Company of Pembroke Works, Ringsend, at £50,000 for rebuilding the front block in Sackville Street. The reconstruction called for Dublin granite and Portland stone dressings as well as one and a quarter million bricks and over a thousand tons of steel. Having acquired at the rear some extra cleared sites, the sides of the G.P.O. were doubled in length to 330 feet and an enclosed shopping arcade linked Princes Street to Henry Street. This unusual arcade was born out of the 1929 reconstruction of the G.P.O. and is an integral part of the main building. It contains several shops including the Philatelic Office which opened in 1975. Incidentally, it was a Dublin man, Henry Archer, who in the 1840s invented a machine to perforate stamp sheets. The narrowness of these two streets rather diminishes the impact and magnificence of the extended building as a whole.

Pillar Boxes

Before 1840, letters for posting had to be delivered to a receiving office, from where they were dispatched by letter carriers to the addressees. The letter carrier had then to knock at the door, wait for a reply and collect the appropriate fee before handing over the mail. The Penny Post, invented by Rowland Hill, revolutionised this cumbersome method by instituting payment at the time of posting. However, many people initially resented having to cut slits in their elegant hall-doors to facilitate acceptance of the letters.

Around this time iron pillar boxes for receiving mail began to appear in Belgium, France and Germany. The novelist Anthony Trollope, who, as Post Office Surveyor or Inspector, had extended rural deliveries in Ireland, was transferred in 1852 to the Channel Islands. He erected a French style pillar box in St Helier and two years later Hill inaugurated the idea in central London. Despite initial public distrust it proved successful, and soon post boxes began to appear in other cities, including Dublin.

With Trollope back in Ireland by 1855, iron receptacles, both free standing and wall mounted, burgeoned all over the country. The ''Penfold'' hexagonal box appeared in 1865, but as many believed that their precious letters got stuck in the corners, the familiar cylindrical shape was adopted 14 years later.

Various efforts were attempted to make them more secure, including a device, ''which will defy attempts of thieves to abstract letters from it, and will also prevent thefts by dishonest postmen by an ingenious system of double connected flaps and doors.''

All boxes prior to 1922 bear the royal insignia of the era. ''V.R.'' represents Queen Victoria up to 1901, ''E.R.'' is King Edward VII, who ruled from 1901 to 1910 and finally ''G.R.'' for King George V, 1910 to Independence in 1921. After 1922 the royal red colour of the pillars was changed to green.

Until recently new pillars had to be imported from Britain, but now they are being manufactured by the Dublin firm of Tonge and Taggart, with the design, tried and tested by time, thankfully unchanged.

POST

COCHRANE
GROVE & CO
DUBLIN

P T

GR

POSTAL
DISTRICT

P T

Arnotts, Henry Street

Henry Street, named after Henry Moore, Earl of Drogheda, was laid down in 1724. Within a hundred years it had firmly established itself as a street of small traders; milliners, apothecaries, cabinetmakers, cutlers, grocers, shoemakers and many others. Into this busy world of small shopkeepers the enterprising duo of George Cannock and Andrew White arrived from Cork in 1843 and bought number 11 to start the drapery firm of Cannock, White & Co.

The flourishing new firm soon acquired numbers 13, 14, 15 and finally number 12 in 1870, which up to then had been a police station. Sir John Arnott injected capital into the business in 1845 and, twenty years later, after Cannock had returned to Limerick, the name changed to John Arnott & Co. In 1875 the firm went public so as to raise money for the hard-pressed Sir John, who had reputedly lost £240,000 in an abortive flour milling venture.

A disastrous fire in 1894 destroyed the group of buildings which formed the store. Within three weeks the company was temporarily operating from the Rotunda Rooms, while the architect, George Beater, built the present structure which additionally took in numbers 9 and 10. The building bristled with Victorian embellishments many of which have since vanished. The partially fluted and decorated cast-iron supporting columns are still an attractive feature of the interior.

Born in Fifeshire in 1814, Sir John Arnott was an entrepreneur, industrialist and philanthropist with a special interest in providing work for the poor. A director of many companies, he also established ship-building yards, bakery shops, mills, factories and even ran a brewery. He was Lord Mayor of Cork 1859-61 and M.P. from 1859-64 and was a prime moving force behind the Irish Poor Law Relief Bill.

In 1874, he bought *The Irish Times* for £35,000 from the widow of the founder Major Lawrence E. Knox. His son became chairman of the newspaper in 1900. This extraordinary man died in 1898.

One of the hallmarks of the city is the rich undulating skyline, seldom more than four or five stories high, punctuated by chimney stacks, church spires, cupolas and the unfortunate intrusion of cranes and some badly designed office blocks. Illustrated above is a rooftop view such as is seen from the top floor of Arnotts.

Number 63 is the Royal Bank branch of Allied Irish Banks. Built in 1869 this is the oldest bank to remain in its original position in the street. The building was modernised in the late 1940s.

The Royal Bank was founded in 1836 by Robert Shaw and the Pim family. Shaw had close links with the milling industry and donated the title deeds of his property in Foster Place for the headquarters of the new bank. Pim, a Quaker, drew his business from fellow religionists and this connection prompted the bank's initial success. The Royal also played a key role in the development of Ireland's first railways.

Number 62, the building which now houses McDonald's Hamburger Restaurant, a worldwide franchising operation, was once the popular Pillar Picture Theatre, and later the Pillar Cafe Restaurant. It was acquired in the late 1970s by the Irish licensees of McDonalds Corporation, Pantry Franchise Ireland Ltd., a company founded by Kerryman Michael Mehigan. The facade has been tastefully restored (as also were those of other branches where they occupied old buildings) and considerable trouble taken in matching the original bricks. The new bricks were eventually obtained in Kingscourt, Co Cavan. The original building had escaped destruction in 1916 and 1922 but, as with the G.P.O., bullet marks can still be seen on the columns.

External advertising has been kept to a minimum and the McDonald's logo does not strike the jarring note of which many plastic signs are guilty.

Next door, at number 61, Flanagans' Steak House, finely complements its neighbour. The refurbishing here is highlighted by the colourful window boxes. Outside the main entrance there is still the almost intact pavement mosaic advertising a former occupier William F. Wells & Son, Pharmaceutical Chemists. Wells and Son were succeeded, in turn by J. J. Roche & Company, also chemists. 13 other shops have mosaics of varying sizes, several of which indicate the names of long-gone businesses.

The premises at number 66, now the Northern Bank, were originally built for an assurance company and they had figures of the Wise and Foolish Virgins, illustrated below, carved in the tympanum as a sober warning to ensure against all eventualities. Walking on the pavement by the bank it is easy, because of the modernised ground floor, to overlook the rich classical lines higher up. The branch was known for many years as Balls Branch, a reference to their predecessor, the privately owned Balls Bank, which the Northern Bank bought at the turn of the century.

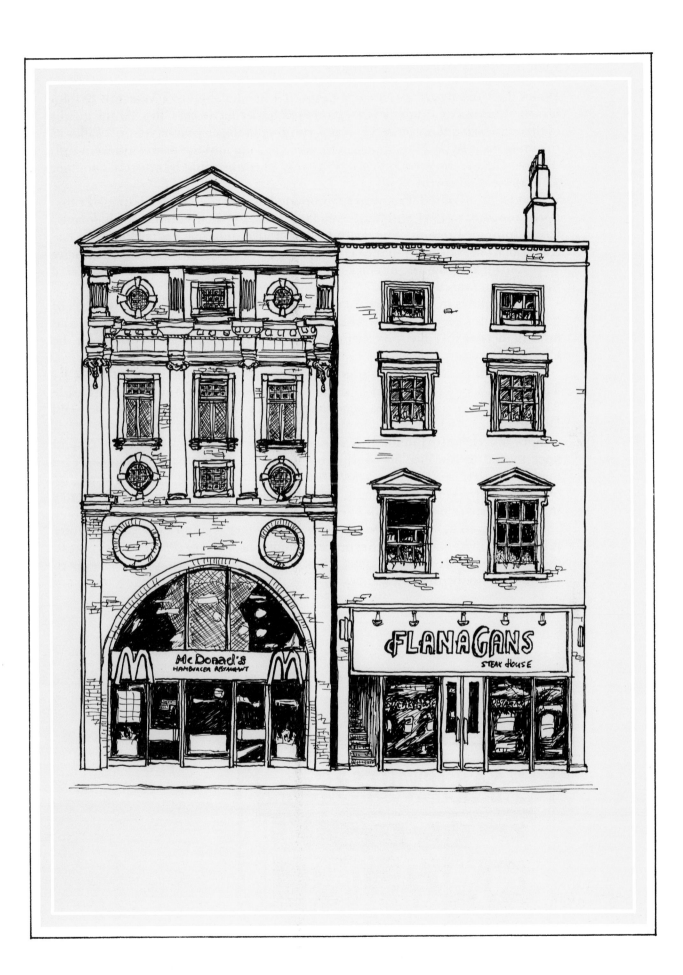

Dublin United Tramway Company

When their old headquarters was destroyed during the Civil War the Dublin United Tramway Company moved into the Sackville Street Club. At the height of their operation there were 330 trams running in the city with Nelson's Pillar as the main hub. By 1925 the bus service was growing and the tramways went into decline. During the Second World War only 91 trams could be mustered and not all of those roadworthy.

The Dublin United Tramways Company became the Dublin United Transport Company in 1941 and four years later was absorbed into the newly formed Córas Iompair Éireann. The death knell sounded only five years later. The last tram ran from Nelson's Pillar to Dalkey 10th July, 1949. The bulk of the vehicles were sold off as outhouses or chicken coops and a few survived to spend the rest of their days in museums.

The tramlines in O'Connell Street, consisted of four parallel lines with six of them opposite Clerys. These were buried intact under a layer of tarmacadam and are still there to this day. Number 59/60 became the management offices for the City Bus Services.

The recent closure of a furniture store revealed again the name of A. & R. Thwaites & Co. Ltd., carved in stone over the entrance to number 57 (beside Marlowe Cleaners). This is a very tangible link with the history of a very old Dublin business which is credited with the invention of soda water.

Ephraim Thwaites founded his apothecary business in Cork Street in 1760 and later moved to number 50 Marlborough Street. While his son Augustine, a medical student in Trinity College, was experimenting in the laboratory, he observed a strange phenomenon, and stumbled across a way to make water bubble and sparkle as never before. Soda water was born!

First believed to have curative powers, soda water has since undergone many refinements in its manufacturing process and it is now a very different beverage to the 18th and 19th century concoctions. There is no plaque on the wall to commemorate the invention.

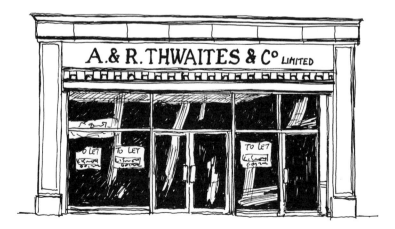

The Carlton Cinema

The Carlton Cinema owes its origin to the Irish National Picture Palace, a long, narrow and dark building which possessed some ornate decoration, a fragment of which has remarkably survived next to the Moore Lane exit of the present structure. Around 1920 the name was changed to the Carlton Cinema and by 1937 some neighbouring premises, including the quaintly named ''Dorset Institution and Repository for Plain and Fancy Needlework'' had been acquired and work commenced on a new 2,000-seat cinema. During construction thousands of intact, but alas empty liquor bottles were discovered in a trench, ingeniously placed there to combat rising damp from the marshy subsoil.

The new Carlton opened on 16th April, 1938, with Cary Grant starring in *The Awful Truth*. Patrons paid their admission at the outside box-office, passed the Celtic-design murals in the vestibule and on entering the auditorium saw on either side of the proscenium arch the beautiful bas-relief panels illustrating orchestral instruments. These features did not survive subsequent reconstruction. Also gone are the elaborate strip neons which once picked out the columns and other architectural highlights on the outside.

In the 1930s and 1940s O'Connell Street on a Saturday night was a carnival of long cinema queues. There were no less than 8 picture houses – including the Rotunda – packing them in. These were: The Savoy, Rotunda, Carlton, Pillar, Capitol, Metropole, Grand Central and the old Astor. Only the first three still survive.

Number 44 was the home of the Irish Meteorological Service until they moved to their futuristic building in Glasnevin. Number 43 was once the headquarters of the Land League and the National League. The Young Mens' Christian Association resided here from 1895 until the fires of 1922 gutted the building. The present owners have recreated a section of railings in front of the building. Two attractive lamp standards have been added giving a nice period tone to the entrance. Even as late as the 1960s many of the buildings along this end of the street were fronted by railings of various designs.

Illustrated below is not a bomb shelter or an entrance to a subway but the descent to the hallowed sanctuary of a gentlemen's lavatory.

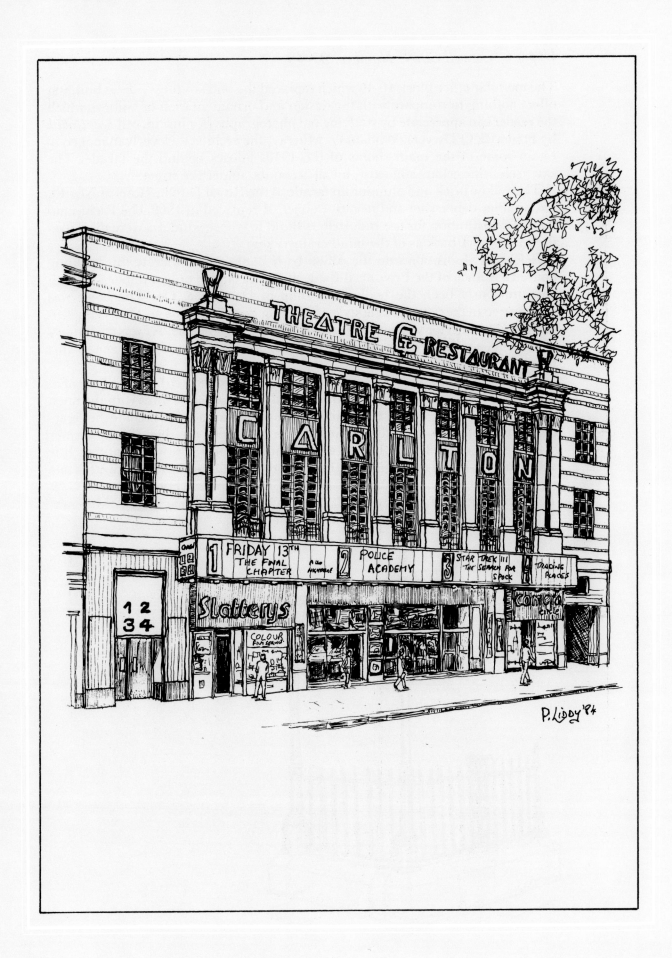

The modular office block 46-49 which replaced the outstanding Gilbeys building offers nothing to compare with the design and ornamentation of Gilbeys which the reader can appreciate by studying old photographs (for instance in *Lost Dublin* by Frederick O'Dwyer). William G. Murray, the architect, cleverly managed to retain some of the main rooms of the 1950s houses behind the facade. The extensive wine cellars still exist, by all accounts, under the street.

The yellow brick and aluminium facade of the Royal Dublin Hotel at No. 40, has a rather depressing and negative effect. It replaced in 1969 The Richmond National Institution for the Industrious Blind in whose windows were displayed the wickerwork baskets of the blind craftworkers.

Before its absorption into the Allied Irish Banks conglomerate this building housed a branch of the Provincial Bank. It first occupied only number 37 which had previously been the booksellers shop of Dawson & Co. The bank was constructed in the neo-classical style employing Portland stone and Ballyknocken granite. The interior walls were lined with Pavonozzi marble. As was customary at the time, a residence was provided in the upper stories for the manager and his family.

The Provincial Bank was founded in 1825 and it pioneered the development of the branch banking system as we know it today. It had close links with the linen industry and the livestock trade. The bank was later extended to include the cigarette factory of John Purcell Ltd. and in the late 1960s number 39, the former headquarters of the Ladies Land League from 1881 to 1882, was acquired. It is almost impossible to distinguish, either from the outside or the inside, any tell tale sign of the two extensions. Original architect, Batchelor and Hicks; Builder, G. & T. Crampton; Steel Work, J. & C. McGloughlin; Wood carving, J. Milligan; Architect last extension, James V. McGrane.

The Gate Theatre

Cavendish Row, formerly Cavendish Street, is named after William Cavendish, the third Duke of Devonshire, who was Viceroy from 1737 to 1745.

The building which now houses the Gate Theatre was designed by Richard Johnston (brother of Francis Johnston) in 1785, as an extension of the Rotunda.

Enclosed by the pediment is the coat of Arms of the Duke of Rutland, after whom the present Parnell Square was originally named. There are two main rooms, one over the other. The lower room was a ballroom and was used as such until relatively recently. In the upper room teas were served and concerts held. The profits from such ventures went to support the hospital.

In 1928, a notice appeared in Dublin: "It is proposed to open the Dublin Gate Theatre Studio in October 1928 for the production of modern and progressive plays unfettered by theatrical convention". Hilton Edwards, Lord Longford and Michael MacLiammoir had come together to form the production team that helped to change the direction of the Irish theatre. Michael Scott, the architect of many well-known buildings, including the modern Abbey Theatre, was engaged to reconstruct the old concert hall in the Rotunda for the use of the new company.

The first production, *Faust* by Goethe, opened on 17th February, 1930. Stage and costume design was by MacLiammoir, and Edwards handled the production and direction. Unfortunately, the heating failed, but the frozen audience was none the less enthusiastic. Since then, The Gate has had many trials and tribulations but also its share of triumphs. Thanks to a grant by the then Minister for Finance, Charles Haughey, T.D., urgent redecorations were undertaken between October 1969 and March 1971. Since then the theatre has been aided by Arts Council grants.

Apart from resident Irish actors, famous names to have appeared at the Gate include Orson Wells and James Mason, the former having to pass a gauntlet of picketers in 1951 when crowds heckled him for being a communist subversive.

Illustrated below is a drinking fountain in Cavendish Row showing the side from which the horses drank — people used the pavement side!

Parnell Square

The growth of Parnell (Rutland) Square began about 1753 when the developer Luke Gardiner and his son Sackville started leasing out plots of land which, up to then, had served as farms. The Rotunda site along Parnell Street (Great Britain Street) had already been acquired by Dr Mosse in 1748 and by 1751 the Gardiners had laid Cavendish Row and North Frederick Street. Pause in the Square for a while to take a closer look at some external features typical of Georgian residences. Many of these were drawn from the west side which has unfortunately become neglected with a large number of the houses remaining unoccupied, decaying or partly demolished. Urgent attention is necessary to retain the integrity of this section.

By 1766, the west side (Granby Row) was opened, followed in 1769 by the northern end (Palace Row). The square soon contained some of the finest residences in Dublin including Ormond House on the east side and Charlemont House, now the Hugh Lane Gallery. Although surrounded by the homes of the working classes and the tenements of the poor, Parnell Square itself remained throughout the 18th and 19th centuries as a highly desirable place to live. With the development of the Rotunda entertainment complex the square became the hub for society activity. This century has seen the gentle transition of the houses from residental to office and institutional uses. The square has remained more or less intact with some recent noteworthy rebuilding on the east side.

The drawing opposite shows the group of buildings at the top of Parnell Square West owned by the Federated Workers' Union of Ireland. The house at the centre was once Vaughan's Hotel, which Michael Collins frequently used as a meeting place during his years on the run.

There is still a look-out box on the first floor landing where his agents spied on the arriving guests. In the gaily decorated back yard there is a surprising and interesting collection of bric-a-brac including railway signals and platform lamps.

Detailed renovations currently being carried out on number 29 graphically reveal that many Georgian mansions were, in fact, jerry-built. The inner course of bricks was laid, at intervals, on horizontal beams of timber. This allows the walls to be raised faster than would be otherwise possible. Unfortunately, the widespread practice (later outlawed by an Act of Parliament) has left a legacy of collapsing floors and has multiplied the costs of restoration.

The footpaths abound in little clues to the pre-reconstruction past and some even go back as far as the days of the grand Georgian mansions. For instance, there are 27 remaining examples of early 19th century coal-hole covers with their elaborate designs all but worn away by age.

The basements under each house once had windows below street level and the open space in front was protected by attractive low walls and railings. Except for numbers 42 & 43 Upper O'Connell Street the railings have all disappeared and the footpaths are extended over the open space. The 178 pavement lights along the street now allow the daylight into these basements.

There are 225 service manholes, of various shapes and sizes, leading to the complexity of giant sewers, water and gas mains and miles of electricity and communications cables. The pavement mosaics which decorate the entrances to several shops have already been mentioned.

Railings and Gates
Some marvellous speciments of the art are to be found in the square, especially in the north and east sides where these two examples are taken from.

P. Liddy '83

Georgian Doorways

No one Georgian doorway, whether in small details or in overall plan, is the same as another. Much has already been written on this subject so I have decided to illustrate only three of the basic designs on which many of the variations are based.

Iron Balconies

The elaborate iron balconies were in the most part Victorian additions and have added a great deal of interest to the otherwise relatively uniform facades.

Footscrapers

The designs of the footscrapers, some of which are very intricate indeed, were as individualistic as the owners of the houses they adorned. The scrapers served an essential function after a walk over muddy footpaths and streets littered with animal traffic.

P. LIDDY '84

31

O'Connell Street Statues

Facing southwards towards O'Connell Bridge, let us briefly look at the statues in the centre of the street.

Parnell Monument

Over 200,000 people followed the funeral of Parnell to Glasnevin Cemetery in 1891 and in the subsequent seven years plans were advanced to erect a monument to the "Chief". Various sites were suggested before settling on the eventual one which was close to Costigan's Hotel from where Parnell, speaking from a window, made his final public speech. It was also assumed that this would be the last statue to be erected in Sackville Street and as such it would be a fitting counterbalance to the O'Connell Monument.

Most of the project finance came from America and some individual contributions approached £3,000. After the necessary rerouting of the tram tracks the foundation stone was laid in October 1899. The eight-foot-high bronze statue was cast in New York and shows Parnell characteristically wearing two overcoats — a sensible arrangement for his draughty perch!

The sculptor was Augustus St-Gaudens, classed as an American but born in Dublin of an Irish mother and a French father. He received £5,000 for the commission.

Twelve years were to pass before a truncated obelisk, surmounted by the eight-foot-high tripod and flame, was completed. John Redmond unveiled the monument in October 1911, a few days off the 20th anniversary of Parnell's death. The ceremony was preceded by a massive procession which took an hour and twenty minutes to pass a point in Grafton Street and such was the swell of the crowd that the protective railings around the monument collapsed.

The base of the obelisk, where, incidentally, many of the surrendering rebels of 1916 laid down their arms, is decorated by a frieze of carved ox skulls which repeats the design around the nearby Rotunda. Inlaid bronze wreaths and plaques carry the names of the provinces and counties of Ireland. An illustration of the march of time is evidenced in the spelling of "Connact" and the naming of Laois and Offaly as Queen's (County) and King's (County).

On the day after the unveiling ceremony Dublin Corporation adopted a resolution to change the name of Great Britain Street to Parnell Street.

Illustrated below are four Victorian cast-iron bollards protecting a manhole cover beside the Parnell Monument. At one time a number of similar groupings were placed at intervals along the length of the street.

Father Theobald Mathew

Father Theobald Mathew was born in 1790 and exactly one hundred years later on 13th October, 1890 the Lord Mayor, E.J. Kennedy, laid the top stone of his monument. The statue itself, sculptured by Miss Mary Redmond, shows the friar dressed in his Capuchin habit which by law he had been proscribed from wearing during his own life time.

He had expended himself in search of justice and relief for the poor and subsequently he became known as the Apostle of Temperance. Before his death he had enrolled into the Temperance Movement about five million members in Ireland and nearly a million in Britain and America.

The consumption of duty paid whiskey in Ireland dropped in 5 years from 12 to 5 million gallons. Roe, the great distiller, sent Father Mathew a cheque for a church he was building saying that no one had done him so much harm, but that the results showed nothing but good for Ireland.

His work suffered severe setbacks after the Famine as the poor in despair turned for consolation to alcohol. Dogged by debt and illness he eventually died at the age of 66.

James Larkin

When the more recent statue of James Larkin, next in line, was unveiled on the 15th June, 1979 its merits were hotly debated, with the oversize hands coming in for the greatest criticism. But the sculptor, the late Oisin Kelly, has since been wholly vindicated and the statue is now accepted as one of the most vibrant in the city, validating Larkin as the giant of the Irish Labour Movement.

The statue, the last to be erected in the street, is appropriately placed in front of Clerys, the site of the former Imperial Hotel. From a balcony window of the hotel in 1913 the defiant Larkin illegally addressed the assembly of striking workers below. This act resulted in a police baton charge which left two dead

and hundreds injured with Larkin himself arrested.

Quotations from Sean O'Casey and Patrick Kavanagh are inscribed on the base of the statue and towards the front is inscribed the quotation "The great appear great because we are on our knees; let us rise".

The erection of the statue, cast by the Dublin Art Foundry, was sponsored by the trade union he founded, The Federated Workers Union of Ireland, which is the second largest in the country.

Nelson's Pillar

An explosion at 1.32 a.m. on Tuesday, March 8th, 1966 ended a 157 year old controversy. City councillors, businessmen and citizens had fiercely argued the pros and cons of the 121 feet high Doric column surmounted by the 13 feet high statue of Horatio Nelson sculpted by Thomas Kirk, R.H.A. But the flash of gelignite made a mockery of argument. For those Dubliners who had procrastinated paying their sixpence and climbing the 166 narrow winding stairs it was now too late. The Pillar, built in 1808, which had become the symbol of the city centre and had been designated the terminus of the tramway system, was now no more.

Sir John Gray

On the island in front of Eason & Son is the statue to Sir John Gray, executed by Thomas Farrell and unveiled in 1879. Gray, a member of Dublin Corporation and proprietor of the *Freeman's Journal,* was mainly responsible for bringing the Vartry water supply to Dublin.

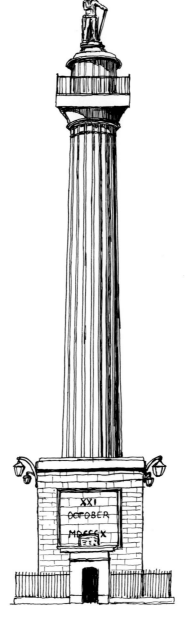

William Smith O'Brien

The statue to William Smith O'Brien was unveiled on 26th December, 1870 at its original site which was across the river near the junction of D'Olier Street and Westmoreland Street. It was removed to its present location, opposite the *Evening Press* in 1929.

Thomas Farrell R.H.A., whose studio was in Lower Gloucester Street, was commissioned to execute the 8 foot high Carrara marble statue. O'Brien is posed addressing an assembly and is shown wearing the contemporary dress of the day; high button waistcoat, frock coat and pantaloons.

The inscription on the base tells of his birth on 17th October, 1803, that he was sentenced to death for high treason on 9th October, 1848 and died 16th June, 1864. O'Brien, who had been a leader of the abortive 1848 Rising, had his death sentence commuted to one of exile to Australia.

The O'Connell Monument

After the funeral of Daniel O'Connell in 1847, a fund to erect a national monument was promoted by several newspapers and the Hierarchy authorised church door collections.

With £8,362 already banked, the two-ton Dalkey granite foundation stone was laid in August 1864. An open competition for a suitable design attracted several entries. In the event, the entry from Dubliner John Henry Foley was accepted. Foley, a sculptor of international reputation, died in 1874, and his assistant Brock completed the work.

On 15th August, 1882 thousands arrived in Dublin from the provinces to celebrate the centenary of the Volunteer Movement and to attend the Industrial and Agricultural Exhibition in the Rotunda Gardens. Overshadowing these events, however, was the unveiling of the almost completed O'Connell monument. The ceremony was performed by the Lord Mayor, and the exuberance of the celebrating throngs, with banners waving and numerous bands playing, was undiminished by the pouring rain.

The overall height of the monument is 40 feet, and the bronze statue of O'Connell wrapped in his famous cloak, is 12 feet high. Immediately underneath is Erin, trampling her cast-off shackles while holding the 1829 Act of Emancipation and pointing to the Liberator. Nearly 30 more figures symbolise the Church, the professions, the arts, the trades and the peasantry. Four winged Victories represent O'Connell's chief virtues. "Patriotism" has a sword in her right hand and a shield in her left. "Fidelity" bears a mariner's compass and strokes a dog. "Eloquence" clasps a sheaf of papers and addresses her listeners. Finally "Courage" is shown strangling a serpent and holding the classic bundle of reeds. Close inspection of "Courage" reveals a bullet hole over her right breast, a legacy 1916-22.

Heraldic House, which as its name implies, provides family Coats of Arms far and wide, is in the first block encountered on the east or left hand side facing southwards. The buildings are undistinguished and not relieved by the non-descript office block which replaced Alex Findlater & Company, Grocery, Wine and Spirit Merchants. Findlaters (established 1823 and in O'Connell Street since 1835) had built cavernous underground cellars said to be capable of storing more hogsheads of wine than could be loaded into the holds of four giant Atlantic liners.

Glancing left down Cathal Brugha Street you can see the College of Catering with three stone ladies portrayed in their corner niche. This institution once housed the College of Domestic Science and the figures represent one girl scrubbing and cleaning, her sitting companion doing embroidery while the remaining figure stands book in hand illustrating that the best way forward is to be equipped with education.

Gresham Hotel

Abandoned as a baby on the steps of the Royal Exchange in London, Thomas M. Gresham became a very successful businessman in Dublin. Rising quickly from the position of household servant to butler he soon acquired enough financial backing to open an hotel.

In 1817 he purchased 21-22 Sackville Street and three years later he leased No. 20. These houses, although united as one building, gave the visiting gentry the seclusion and comfort of a town house allied to the service of a first class hotel. Acclaimed internationally, the hotel was patronised by many of the royal and noble families of Europe.

In order to concentrate on his commercial interests in Kingstown (Dun Laoghaire) which included the Royal Marine Hotel, Gresham sold his Dublin hotel in 1865 to a group of Cork businessmen. Various alterations and improvements were commissioned and in 1906 a concert and dining hall was constructed.

Two hundred guests were trapped in the hotel during the Rising of 1916. Food almost ran out both for them and the contingent of British Army snipers placed on the roof to fire on the G.P.O. By the end of the hostilities much of the street lay in ruins, but the Gresham remained intact.

Michael Collins, who once narrowly escaped capture when confronted in the hotel dining room by the dreaded Auxiliaries, led the post-Treaty negotiations between the I.R.A. and the British Army in the Gresham. Black clouds were gathering, however, and when anti-Treaty forces under Cathal Brugha occupied the building in July 1922, the whole block was reduced to rubble by Government troops. Of the five hotels in the block only the Gresham was rebuilt. Nineteen O'Connell, next to the Gresham Hotel, has the distinction of being the only pub in the street.

Savoy Cinema

The Savoy Cinema was opened on the 29th November, 1929 by President Cosgrave and the occasion, according to the souvenir programme, "marked another step forward in the entertainment of the city". The cinema had the most up to date equipment of the time and was lavishly decorated in a Venetian style. The opening film was *On with the Show* billed as the first 100% natural colour film to be screened in Ireland.

During the war years the big hits of the day helped to distract people's minds from the gloom and the rationing. In 1942 special excursions brought filmgoers from all over the country to see *Gone with the Wind*. Its run was only eight weeks long but in that time the 3,000 seat auditorium gave around 300,000 patrons the opportunity of seeing the film.

St John Ambulance Brigade First Aid Post

The St John Ambulance Brigade was founded in Ireland in 1903 by Sir John Lumsden (who also founded the Royal Dublin Golf Club). The first division operated from the Guinness Brewery at St James' Gate.

After the street riots of the 1913 General Strike a permanent post was established in O'Connell Street on a site granted to the Brigade by the Dublin United Tramway Company. The post, and, of course, the whole Brigade organisation, gave sterling service during the 1916 Rising, the subsequent Troubles and the Civil War. Combatants on both sides were unselfishly ministered to by the medical volunteer members who inevitably suffered casualties themselves.

During both World Wars but more especially during the 1914-18 conflict, before the Knights of Malta and the Red Cross had been introduced into Ireland, thousands flocked to the ranks of the Brigade and served at home and abroad. Most major firms in the city had their own in-house divisions.

In the wake of the civil commotions, military repressions and rebel insurgencies of the 1920s many of Dublin's poorer classes were near starvation. The Brigade responded by setting up meal centres to offer pregnant women and their families an adequate balanced diet. Their work was so successful in saving lives that the scheme was keenly studied by the equally hard-pressed Germans and later, in 1929, by the depression-hit Americans.

The O'Connell Street post used to be staffed day and night but is now open only to serve parades, rallies and other festive or sporting occasions. The present hut is a recent replacement containing every first aid facility and was donated by Arthur Guinness and Son as a token of their long association with the Brigade.

SAVOY 1 SPLASH 2 BREAKDANCE 3 AGAINST ALL ODDS 4 EDUCATING RITA 5 UNDER FIRE

Splash

The Oonnell Florist

P. Liddy '84

41

Marlborough Street

Any pretensions to grandeur that Marlborough Street might have once possessed were dispelled when the peers and gentry of the district fled to avoid the encroaching slums of the 19th century. By the turn of the century at least three pawnbroking establishments offered their services along the street. Carthy's, occupying the former town house of Lord Marlborough, is the sole survivor of the three.

Next door to Carthy's, at the corner of Cathedral Street, is the old head-quarters of the now defunct North City Loan and Investment Society. Tyler's shoe repair shop, established in the 1920s, continues to trade on the ground floor. Cathedral Street itself was at one time only a service lane to the back gardens of the North Earl Street houses.

The Pro-Cathedral was begun in 1816 under Archbishop Troy and finished in 1825 under Archbishop Murray. Dr Troy had hoped for the G.P.O. site but fear of Protestant opposition forced him to pick the more secluded ground of the recently vacated Lord Annesley's house.

The architect was probably an amateur, John Sweetman, but there are some who also credit George Papworth or John Taylor. In any event all three had some on-site involvement.

The extensive vaults of the church, which run under the street to the Department of Education, contain nearly a thousands remains, including those of Dr John Charles McQuaid, the late Archbishop of Dublin. The vaults were once leased to the Government as a whiskey store in order to earn revenue for the building fund.

John McCormack joined the church's Palestrina Choir in 1907 and, recognising his talent, the choirmaster gave him the instruction and encouragement which helped to launch him on to the world stage.

No application has ever been made to elevate St Mary's Pro-Cathedral to the status of a full cathedral. Christ Church was constituted by the Pope as the city's cathedral church and, although Protestant since the Reformation, this decision has never been revoked.

The Angelus bell rung by R.T.E. is the bell of the Pro-Cathedral.

John Keys' little tobacconist shop (illustrated below) has changed little in the last 60 years. Hammam Buildings, housing the offices of the Inspector of Taxes, derives its name from the defunct Hammam Hotel and Turkish Baths.

P. Liddy '83

The Kylemore Bakery arrived in O'Connell Street about 1934, but the firm opened for business in 1887 and their first shop was the one still at 73 Talbot Street. There are now 30 branches in the city supplying the needs of thousands of workers for their morning tea breaks. Notice the sunblind which, at one time, was a feature of nearly every shop in the city. Now it only graces some food and drapery shops.

McDowells at number 3 was established in 1870 and moved to Sackville Street in 1904. The shop was looted and burnt in 1916 but was quickly rebuilt, the contractors using salvaged girders from the gutted shell of the G.P.O. The Architect was F. Bergin and the contractors Shortall & Co. The owner, Jack McDowell was suddenly catapulted to fame in 1947 when his horse, Caughoo, an outsider at 100 to 1, ran the race of his life and won the Aintree Grand National. A heavy mist had seriously restricted visibility and Caughoo's runaway victory was only evident towards the final stages of the race. This gave rise to the saying ''out of the mist like the racehorse Caughoo'' to describe an unexpected happening. The horse had been bought for only 50 guineas six years earlier and was trained by Jack's brother, Herbert. The victors' boat journey home after the race achieved an entry into the first *Guinness Book of Records*. Toasting Caughoo, the McDowells bought all and sundry the world's largest round of drinks!

Old traditions and trimmings have been faithfully preserved in the shop. For instance, you can still hand in a watch and have it repaired in the same premises by the craftsmen upstairs. Antiquity is honoured by the gas lamps hanging from the ceiling and still connected to the mains. Generations of engaged couples have come to McDowells to select their rings. Country couples used first buy the ring and then repair to Wynns Hotel in Lower Abbey Street for a celebratory meal. The decorative advertising on the front wall is claimed to have been the first animated neon sign in Ireland.

Messrs William Lawrence and Son had a photographic and toy shop on the site now occupied by Prosperity Chambers at numbers 5 and 7. A journeyman photographer, Robert French, worked for Lawrence and he recorded on glass plates thousands of turn-of-the-century scenes of Dublin and the rest of Ireland. This invaluable work, known as the Lawrence Collection, is now in the custody of the National Library. As the shop was also a toy emporium it was a particular target for wanton looting and subsequent burning in 1916. Burtons, numbers 1 and 2 at the corner with North Earl Street, was built by Tylers Shoes as a substitute for their demolished shop. Architects, O'Callaghan and Webb.

At the corner with North Earl Street is Best Ltd., menswear, which was the former site of Nobletts, wholesale confectioners, and one of the first buildings to be looted during the Easter Rising. As soon as law and order broke down young and old from nearby tenements were seen stuffing themselves with sweets and chocolates while remaining totally oblivious to the deadly crossfire from snipers.

Next door, number 33, another casualty of the uprising, was rebuilt for Jameson and Co. Ltd., jewellers.

The musical clock, displaying figures representing King Lir and his metamorphic daughters, fell silent a few years ago. It seems that all efforts to have its unique mechanism repaired have so far been fruitless, which is a great pity as the chimes added a pleasant note to the cacophany of the passing traffic.

Saxone Shoe Company occupies at number 31 the original site of the Munster and Leinster Bank before it moved to the corner of Lower Abbey Street. Adjoining Saxone's is Kinahans, a successor to O'Farrells, a tobacco, snuff and foreign cigar importer.

The Saxone and Kinahan buildings were erected in 1919 and Irish granite was used on the facade. Architects, Moore, Keefe, Donnelly and Robinson; Contractors, G. & T. Crampton and J. & C. McGloughlin.

The motto in the finely carved porchway of the Bank of Ireland reads: "Bona Fides Reipublicae Stabilitas". The literal translation is "Good Faith is the Cornerstone of the State" which transposes into the notion that you can rely on the bank to safeguard your money.

Pre 1916, this was the site of Richard Allen's, tailors for gentlemen, who also specialised in supplying livery for servants and chauffeurs. Architects, McDonnell and Dixon, Ely Place; Stone Carving, J. Harrison and Son; Contractors, J. & P. Good.

Clerys

On 29th November, 1940, while Europe was reeling from the hammer blows struck by Nazi Germany, Dubliners throned the streets around the re-opening Clery's Department Store. A few months earlier the store had gone into liquidation. Fears about its future were dispelled when the legendary Denis Guiney bought the business and launched a new company Clery & Co (1941) Ltd with a massive share capital of £250,000.

Eighty-seven years earlier Peter Paul McSwiney and John Delaney had built their "New Mart" next door to the Imperial Hotel. In time, the hotel and drapery store shared the same extended building with the retail business confined to the ground floor. McSwiney, a successful and charitable businessman, became Lord Mayor in 1864 and in that year laid the foundation stone of the Round Tower Monument to Daniel O'Connell in Glasnevin Cemetery.

Following the eventual retirement of both co-founders the name of the store was changed in 1882 to "The Dublin Drapery Warehouse Co Ltd," a company which lasted only fifteen months before being wound up by Mr Robert Gardner of Craig Gardner and Co. (who were also the 1940 liquidators).

M.J. Clery, a native of Kilmallock, Co Limerick, bought the premises and stock for £32,000 in November, 1883. Clery's career was an eminently accomplished one, but his personal life was stricken with tragedy. By the time he himself had died of a heart attack in 1896 he had already buried his first wife and six of his eight children had succumbed to tuberculosis.

Clery's successors witnessed the total destruction of their property in 1916, but within two months they were in business again in the Metropolitan Building in Lower Abbey Street. In 1920 the foundation stone of the impressive present building, designed by Ashlin and Coleman of Dawson Street, was laid and two years later the new premises were opened. A main feature of the interior was a water fountain in the centre aisle, from which radiated the various departments. Overhead, there was an unrestricted view of the surrounding Grand Gallery and the elegant glass-panelled ceiling.

The estimate for rebuilding was £87,867.

Tucked away in the adjacent porch is an old door leading downstairs to a ladies and gents hairdressers. This was once the basement establishment of W. Macken where I personally remember seven or eight barbers wielding their scissors and razors and applying hot towels and Brylcreem to produce the conservative styles of the 1950s and 1960s. No matter how busy it was the barbers unerringly knew which customer was first in line.

Lower O'Connell Street, Numbers 9-17

The Irish Permanent has occupied the former Hibernian Bank premises since 1953. This is an exceptionally fine corner building generously adorned with carvings and embellishments. The public area, a legacy of the old banking hall, is particularly striking. Architect, W.H. Byrne and Sons.

In the same block are two buildings which were designed in the 1920s as office blocks and still perform the same function. Unity Buildings (number 16/17) sports a large iron balcony and its near neighbour is the American Chambers, so called because the offices of the United States Consulate were located here for several years. These buildings were built in 1917. Architect, George L. O'Connor; contractor, T.P. Donnell and Sons.

This corner with Lower Abbey Street was rebuilt by the Munster and Leinster Bank in 1922. The facade is described as a free form of classical Renaissance. The inside is also a wonderful riot of classicism with an unexpected glazed and ironwork dome supported by Irish-marbled pillars. The light coloured polished stone gives an airy ambience to the otherwise heavy ornamentation.

The previous building housed the Irish School of Wireless and the rebels used the equipment to broadcast the 1916 Rising to the world. Architect, McDonnell and Dixon; contractors, J. & H. Martin; plasterwork, George Rome & Co.; bronze and strongroom work, J. & C. McGloughlin.

Allied Irish Banks

The Munster and Leinster Bank was founded in Cork mainly at the instigation of James J. Murphy of brewing fame. The specialisation of the bank in its early days was towards the agricultural co-operative movements and the public authorities.

In 1966 it was amalgamated with the Provincial Bank and the Royal Bank but at this stage each bank retained its own day-to-day identity. Six years later they were integrated fully under the title "Allied Irish Banks Ltd".

There are now 254 branches in the Republic, 38 in Northern Ireland, 35 in Britain and one each in the Isle of Man, the Channel Islands and Singapore. The group will attain a controlling interest by 1988 of the huge First Maryland Bankcorp of Baltimore, U.S.A.

Next door to the bank is Cassidy Silks Ltd., which was once the offices of architect Frederick W. Higgenbotham. When the building was destroyed he lost no time in designing the replacement and the Grand Central Cinema two doors down the street.

Lower Abbey Street

V.H.I. Building

The general site of the V.H.I. building itself is historic and formed part of the area occupied by the great mediaeval Cistercian Abbey of Saint Mary (from which Abbey Street gets its name). The land was a huge salt marsh until early 18th century reclamations and the building of quay walls to contain the Liffey encouraged the eastward spread of the city. One of the earliest buildings of significance along this stretch of Abbey Street was the Northumberland Baths, one of Dublin's first public baths. The present structure dates from 1900 when the paper mechants, Messrs. Armstrong, founded the Northumberland works. In May 1915 a disastrous fire gutted the building and only through supreme effort was the church next door saved. It provided the city's fire fighting forces with a timely rehearsal for the calamities 11 months later, in Easter Week 1916.

The Dunlop Tyre Company bought the ruined shell, discovered that the stout walls were completely sound, and entirely refurbished the building to appear much as it is today. In 1967 the V.H.I. became the new owners.

The small church, neatly tucked in beside the V.H.I. building bears the curious title of the Ormond Quay and Scots Church. It was built in 1866 to accommodate the city's Presbyterian congregation of Scottish shipbuilding and engineering workers.

They were joined in 1938 by the Ormond Quay congregation, a group which could trace their history back to an original foundation in 1661 in the then fashionable Bull Alley. Only the lower portion of the front elevation of their church in Ormond Quay now remains, a sad reminder of the days when the building boasted a sumptuously-timbered interior where each pew had its own little door to keep out the draughts.

Salvation Army

Thirteen Lower Abbey Street is the Dublin headquarters of the Salvation Army.

Built originally as a Congregational Chapel, it was bought for the Army in 1910 and opened for worship in 1913. It is now the chief administrative base of the Army in the Republic and a centre for community work in the city. 1913 was, of course, the year of the great strike in Dublin, a time of cruel injustices and crushing poverty for the working classes. The Salvation Army carried out much charitable work among the homeless, exploited and starving.

The Sally Army, as the Army was affectionately known by Dubliners, came down from Belfast to Dublin in 1884. This was only about 20 years after the founder, William Booth, a pawnbroker by profession, started his Christian Mission. In 1878 the Christian Mission became known as The Salvation Army and by the time the organisation arrived in Dublin it was firmly established in many countries around the world.

52

Lower O'Connell Street, Numbers 1-7

The poet Percy Bysshe Shelley stayed for two months in a house which at one time stood on the site of the present Bank of Ireland, and once addressed a gathering on the street below from an upstairs window. It was probably the extraordinary structure of the Dublin Bread Company Restaurant which replaced the house. It is easy to recognise this distinctive building in old photographs with its incongruous and dominating lantern-like tower. Ravaged by the fires of 1916, the shell was torn down and replaced in 1923 by the Dublin Bread Company Picture House which later evolved into the Grand Central Cinema. A glass canopy (built by J. & C. McGloughlin) once extended all the way across the wide footpath but three months after erection a bomb temporarily put it out of commission. The canopy was later removed altogether. The Hibernian Bank, now part of the Bank of Ireland group, took over occupancy in 1942. Architect, F.W. Higgenbotham.

After the destruction of this block Hamilton Long moved from number three to number five, taking over the lease of the Great Western Railway of England and rebuilding with the compensation that was received. The firm is a long established one; there is a record of a patent to manufacture soda water granted to W.F. Hamilton in 1809. It became a limited company in 1880.

Until fairly recent times some staff lived in and could be called on for urgent prescriptions by ringing a bell after hours.

The Waverly Hotel and Restaurant has given way to the classical lines of the Ulster Bank. The ground floor although modernised tends to emphasise the elegant upper floors and the dome. This was the last building in the block to be rebuilt after 1916 and is dated 1923. Architect, James Hanna C.E.; architectural ornament, C.W. Harrison and Sons. (They also worked on Clerys, Hibernian Bank and the Grand Central Cinema).

November 1975 saw the Irish Nationwide Building Society taking over number 1 from the watchmakers and jewellers, Hopkins and Hopkins, who had traded here for generations. The previous building to this one was a rebel stronghold in 1916 and as a result was shattered by British shellfire.

A reminder of the past era was thoughtfully preserved by the Irish Nationwide when they purchased a magnificant timepiece from Hopkins and Hopkins which is now proudly displayed in the front window. Architect, O'Callaghan & Webb.

The Liffey Ferry and Custom House Quay

The opening of the new toll bridge in 1984 finally snuffed out a 319-year-old tradition of the Liffey ferries between North Wall and Ringsend and South Wall. The craft, with its noisy diesel engine, quaint steering wheel, rudder cables and other nautical paraphernalia, was surprising spacious, and a generation or two ago it was quite common to carry a crew of 2 and 60 passengers on a single crossing. Recently the ferry operated on demand and often carried no more than one hundred passengers a day. The ferry was suspended in stormy weather and whenever the swell made it unsafe to step on board from the slippery quay-side steps.

My drawing shows the number nine ferry, on its way to take up station, passing the Custom House Quay and the entrance to St George's Dock. Situated only a stone's throw away from the Custom House, the massive lift bridge and its sea locks today lie idle, but are still serviceable. The dock, along with a second inner basin, was built to afford shelter to the myriads of sailing ships which frequented the port in its heyday, especially during the late 18th century.

When Oliver Cromwell and his 13,000 Roundheads invaded Ireland they had to land at Ringsend as there were no suitable docking facilities further inland. Then, early in the 18th century, the North and South Walls were built. These were followed by the Custom House Quay which, with the lift bridge and St George's Dock, cost £300,000, a staggering sum for those days.

A few hundred yards further downriver is a second lift bridge. This spans the entrance to the Royal Canal.

On Sunday 21st October, 1984 the service closed with free trips for the crowds who had gathered to watch the opening of the new toll bridge across the Liffey linking Fairview to Ringsend.

The Guinness Ships

The Guinness ships, berthing at City Quay, have been part of the Dublin scene since 1913. In that year the brewery acquired its first ship, the SS W.M. Barkley, which enabled the firm to expand the export side of the business. Unfortunately, the Barkley was torpedoed in 1917 and sank with the loss of five lives. A succession of ships followed, including the SS Carrowdore, which almost became Guinness' second war casualty. In 1941 it miraculously escaped destruction when a 550lb bomb ricochetted off the forecastle and exploded in the sea.

Many Dubliners will remember the fleet of steampowered barges which transported the wooden casks of stout from Victoria Quay, opposite the brewery downriver to the waiting ships. Their funnels were hinged so that at high tide they could pass unscathed under the bridges. The venerable old craft were retired in 1961 and, although I am not certain of their location, one or two may still be operating as sand barges on Lough Neagh.

Large transportable steel tanks, which replaced the wooden casks, were hauled by road during the 1960s and early 1970s to Guinness' specially constructed ships; MV The Lady Grania, MV The Lady Patricia. The MV The Lady Patricia was converted to a bulk liquid tanker in 1973, and the other two vessels were phased out soon after the arrival in 1976 of the world's first custom-built bulk liquid carrier, the MV Miranda Guinness. She was hailed as a spectacular technological breakthrough and enquiries about her were received from many overseas countries.

The ships are now loaded direct from road tankers which carry the equivalent of 130 barrels. It takes 50 tanker loads to fill the fifteen tanks on each ship, which is enough stout to pour nearly two million pints.

Sailing out with the high tide, the journey time to Runcorn, near Liverpool, is 14 hours. On the return journey, the 12 man crew is kept busy steam cleaning the empty tanks and the miles of pipework in readiness for the next consignment.

The Liffey Bridges from O'Connell Bridge

A bronze plaque on the bridge relays the following information: "Carlisle Bridge built in 1794. Rebuilt by the Dublin Port and Docks Board 1880. Renamed O'Connell Bridge by the Municipal Council 1880. Right Hon. Edmund Dwyer Gray M.P. Lord Mayor, James W. Mackey High Sheriff, Binden B. Stoney Engineer, W.J. Doherty Contractor".

The breaking of a bottle of champagne for the rechristening and reopening took place on the 6th May, 1880.

When John Beresford developed the new Custom House in 1791 and three years later opened Carlisle Bridge across a former ferry crossing, the resultant effects were profound and dramatic and were felt almost immediately. The main north-south axis of the city moved further downstream, new roads radiated out from this latest bridge, stimulating the growth of great Georgian squares and avenues on the south side. Only the aristocracy living along Sackville and Grafton Streets felt uneasy, as their elegant thoroughfares gradually surrendered to an invasion of commercial institutions.

The bridge named after Frederick, the fifth Earl of Carlisle, a poet and friend of Byron, was designed by James Gandon.

In 1880, the Dublin Port and Docks Board replaced Gandon's hump-backed, narrow structure with a near replica, except that it was now virtually level and, with a breadth of 155 feet, has the distinction of being nearly as wide as it is long. Portions of Gandon's bridge still survive in the most unlikely places. The balustrade graces the front wall of Clonturk House for the Adult Blind in Drumcondra, and the original keystone heads, carved by the sculptor Edward Smyth, were removed to a premises on Sir John Rogerson's Quay. The new heads were carved by C.W. Harrison.

In the past some remarkable events have taken place on this site. The corpses of insurgents swung from a builder's scaffolding in the aftermath of the 1798 Rising. An altogether more sanctifying occasion took place in 1932 when Benediction was celebrated from the specially constructed altar during the Eucharistic Congress.

An unattractive concrete flower bed was laid along the centre in 1953 to inaugurate An Tóstal, an annual festival which petered out in Dublin within a few years. A contraption called a Bowl of Light surmounted the arrangement, part of which was later thrown into the Liffey by a student. The late Jimmy O'Dea had solemnly proclaimed the concrete lump to be the "Tomb of the Unknown Gurrier."

Thankfully it has since been removed and the elegant three-branched lamps, illustrated below, replaced it.

60

The Ha'penny Bridge

The Ha'penny Bridge is one of Dublin's most famous landmarks and its neatly curved silhouette has often been featured, from books and postcards to television documentaries. It is certainly one of the most popular Liffey crossings for pedestrians, conveniently connecting the Henry Street/Abbey Street areas to the commercial southside. Originally built as the Wellington Bridge in 1816, the cast-iron structure became quickly known as the Ha'penny Bridge when this amount was the toll charged to cross it. At each end of the bridge there are railed side platforms where the toll collectors sat. The turnstiles were removed and the bridge declared open to the public on the 25th March, 1919.

Liffey Street, on the north side of the river, is the weekly arena for that indomitable Dubliner, Hector Grey. Now in his late 70s, he has conducted his special brand of open-air market every Sunday morning for 53 years. Behind Hector's soap box stands the Victorian canopied premises of the Dublin Woollen Company. James Joyce once contracted himself to sell Irish tweed in Trieste on behalf of the firm. Alas, his venture proved unsuccessful. The bridge itself has for generations been the busking ground for numerous fiddlers, penny whistlers and the occasional blind accordionist.

The bridge has also an association with Sir Hugh Lane. In 1913 he conceived the idea of a Bridge Art Gallery and had the famous English architect, Sir E.L. Lutyens, draw up plans to "replace the ugly metal footbridge" with a colonnaded structure. Lane offered to pay half of the building costs to the Corporation, who were looking for a site for the Municipal Art Gallery at the time, but his proposal was not accepted.

On the south side the bridge leads to the Merchants' Arch, one of the few arched lanes left in Dublin. The arch forms part of the Merchant Tailors Guild Hall. It was commissioned in 1821 when the guild vacated the old Tailors Hall in Back Lane. It was designed by Francis Darley who later became the Trinity College architect from 1834. The Ha'penny Bridge has just undergone an extensive renovation carried out by Dublin Corporation and is now floodlit at night-time.

P.LIDDY '82

Liffey Bridges, Upriver

Grattan Bridge (Capel Street) in the foreground of Sunlight Chambers had two predecessors. The first was founded by the Earl of Essex, Arthur Capel, in 1676 but it collapsed 10 years later. The second bridge featured a large equestrian statue of King George I. The Port and Docks Board built the present decorative structure in 1875 which is neatly topped by six exquisite lamps.

O'Donovan Rossa Bridge (Winetavern Street)
Built in 1813, following on from Capel Street Bridge, was originally named Richmond Bridge. It features 6 carved heads. The 3 on the East side are; Plenty, Anna Livia and Industry. Their West side companions are: Commerce, Hibernia and Peace.

Father Mathew Bridge (Bridge Street-Church Street)
This is, in one sense, Dublin's most historic ground as it is the site of the Hurdle Ford — Baile Átha Cliáth. The first stone bridge was erected here about 1210 by the Normans and was so wide that it accommodated houses and shops on it. Destroyed during the Bruce Invasion of 1317 it was not rebuilt until 1380. The present bridge dates from 1816 and was re-christened in 1938 from Whitworth Bridge to mark the centenary of the Temperance Movement.

Liam Mellowes Bridge (Queen Street-Bridgefoot Street)
Formerly known as Arran Bridge, built 1776, this is the oldest existing bridge. It replaced a 1683 structure. Initially it was called Queen's Bridge after the wife of King George III and was subsequently named Bridewell Bridge, and Ellis Bridge and then the aforementioned names.

Rory O'More Bridge (Watling Street)
The Liffey ferrymen violently objected to the opening in 1670 of the original bridge as they feared that their livelihood would be seriously threatened. Their encounter with the forces of the law and order gained the crossing the nickname of Bloody Bridge. The present iron bridge was opened in 1863 and in recent times the name 'Victoria' was dropped in favour of the 1641 rebellion leader Rory O'More.

Seán Heuston Bridge (Kingsbridge)
Built in 1827 to a design of George Papworth and originally named Kingsbridge to honour the state visit of King George IV to Dublin. Papworth was also the designer of Whitefriar Street church.

Sunlight Chambers, Parliament Street

Sunlight Chambers is probably one of the most photographed buildings in Dublin but, paradoxically, it is also one of the least documented. It stands at the river end of Parliament Street and its longer side stretches along Wellington Quay. It was built at the turn of the century and replaced a group of shops, including the premises of Mason Instruments (established in 1813 and still trading elsewhere in the city).

It was built by Lord Leverhulme of Lever Brothers as his Irish head-office. This period saw a great increase in the sales and promotion of all branded products, especially soap. The trade name for Lever Brothers soap was Sunlight, hence the name Sunlight Chambers.

As part of their education and advertising programme the soap company decided to commission a series of panels placed over the ground and first floor windows, depicting the story of soap. These friezes were sculpted in terracotta and coloured. They illustrate the extraction of raw material for soap, merchants buying and selling oils, and manufacturing processes. The everyday use of soap is represented by women using scrubbing boards and visiting washing rooms. Four of the panels remain unfinished.

The building, with its friezes and Italianate architecture, is more remarkable outside than in, but it does boast a fine wooden balustraded staircase. After Lever Brothers moved, it was occupied in turn by the Revenue Commissioners, the Racing Board, and is presently owned by a firm of solicitors.

The Sunlight Chambers is on the Corporation's Protected Buildings list.

Fishamble Street

Many of the streets of old Dublin were originally named after the main trade carried on in the locality. Some existing examples are Cornmarket, Haymarket, Merchants Quay and Winetavern Street. Fishamble Street got its name from the fish markets which once thrived there.

In 1356, the government of the day found it necessary to order that fish were to be sold only at the Fishambles. Fish was a vital part of the citizens' diet and unscrupulous dealers had been charging exorbitant prices. The new order fixed prices and offenders were punished with imprisonment.

Fishamble Street became a very fashionable residential area and many distinguished 17th and 18th century figures lived here, including Henry Grattan. At one time the G.P.O. moved here from High Street and printing houses and taverns also abounded.

The street is best known today for its musical connections with George Frederick Handel. The world premier of *Messiah* with Handel himself conducting, was performed in Mr Neil's new Musick Hall on 13th April, 1742. The composer's masterpiece was well received by the audience who appreciated the privileges bestowed on the second city of the empire. The ladies had been asked to "discard their hoopskirts and gentlemen their swords in order to make more room for the public". Handel, suffering disappointment in London, had come to Dublin "to offer this generous and polished nation something new".

Today the site of the Music Hall is taken by the ironworks of Kennan & Sons. This firm was established in 1770 and is one of the oldest manufacturing companies in continuous business in the city. The main workshop features three different levels, which obviously corresponded to the seating arrangements in the Music Hall. One hopes that Kennans carry on their fine tradition on such an historic site. Across the road, the new Civic Offices are almost complete and they will radically alter the character of the winding Fishamble Street. Whether this will enhance or detract from the area remains to be seen.

Irish Distillers, Smithfield

Across the river, the Smithfield area was already renowned for its half dozen or so distilleries by 1780 when John Jameson bought a controlling interest in his uncle's distillery in Bow Street. Whiskey was probably first introduced into Ireland around the 14th century after Irish monks learned the process of distillation from the Arabs. At first the Uisce Beatha was solely used for medicinal purposes.

However, by the 16th century whiskey drinking had clearly become very popular; an Act of 1556 referred to aqua vitae as being drunk "universally throughout the realm of Ireland." There are also numerous accounts from the 16th and 17th centuries of Irish whiskey being specially sent to gentry and government officials in England where it was obviously highly appreciated.

The giant distillery in Bow Street was closed in 1972, when the Midleton complex was opened by Irish Distillers, the company formed as a result of the merger of Jameson's, Power's and Cork Distillers. The old spirit store at Smithfield became the group administration headquarters in 1980. The building had to be completely restored and the simple strong lines of its limestone exterior were complemented by tasteful landscaping. Cask winches, pot stills and other paraphernalia are preserved on this site.

Overhead pipelines, which once connected the spirit store with the main distillery, pumped the precious liquid into oak casks which were then stored until the spirit was matured. Oak casks are still used today and the traditional cooper's art has been kept alive. The walls of the nearby boiler house, with its huge chimney, were once a draw for some of the city's homeless men. Here they could spend a chilly day leaning against what was called the "hot wall".

Smithfield itself was laid out at the end of the 17th century as the city's cattle market and remained so until 1886. Currently the "square" is being landscaped by the Corporation using traditional cobblestones for the retaining walls.

Thundercut Alley, Smithfield

One of the few remaining of the alleyways that once festooned the city especially in the environs of the Liffey. Their disappearance is not only removing their unique character, but many of the city's oldest street names are in danger of dying with them.

Of these curious Dublin street names, some, thankfully, still live on: Roper's Rest, Misery Hill, Usher's Island, Marrowbone Lane, Hoggen Green (College Green), Minchin's Mantle (Kildare Street), Cow Parlour, Behind Street, Horseman's Row, Cross Poddle, Long Entry and Crooked Staff (Ardee Street).

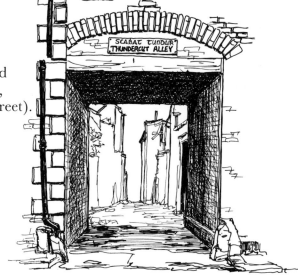

P. Liddy '83

St Audoen's and the Old City Walls

A spear's throw from Wood Quay is a hill which is the very site of the birthplace of Dublin. This hallowed ground stretches from Christ Church to the view in the drawing. The hill overlooked a natural harbour formed by the convergence of the River Poddle with the Liffey Estuary and was known as Dubh-Linn, or the Black Pool. The early Irish settlement here gave way, first to the Danes, and then to the Normans. The latter enclosed the whole town with massive walls and as many as 32 fortified gates, keeps and castles. Today, the only substantial remains of these walls are in Cook Street.

This section of wall was built in 1240. St Audoen's Arch, its main gate, was completed in 1275. St Audoen was named after Bishop Owen, Patron Saint of Rouen; Fagan's Gate, the smaller postern gate, was called after Fagan's Castle, a strongpoint which stood here. When reclaimed land pushed back the Liffey this stretch of wall fell into decay.

The high tower belongs to St Audoen's, the oldest continuously used parish church in Dublin. Founded in 650, parts of this building date from 1190. The tower contains six bells, one of which, at least, was cast in 1423. A public appeal has just been launched to finance essential repairs to the tower. The church in the background is the "new" Catholic church of St Audoen's, built in 1846.

In 1880, the Corporation planned to demolish St Audoen's Arch but public outrage forced them to restore it. Our present day Corporation deserve credit for their restoration work on the walls carried out for the European Architectural Heritage Year in 1975.

The Parks Department have since extended the line of the original wall with limestone boulders and have landscaped the whole area. The upper enclosure, St Audoen's Park, is bounded by low railings, which were salvaged from the demolition of the old city Cattle Market. In recognition of their transformation of an old derelict site into an attractive historical park, the Corporation received an award in 1982 from Bord Fáilte and the Irish Town Planning Institute.

St Audeon's Arch

P. Liddy '82

73

Brazen Head Inn (Bridge Street)

This is one of the most charming little nooks in the whole of the city and is rightly a place of pilgrimage both for the thirsty working man and the enthusiastic amateur historian.

The Brazen Head, the oldest pub in Ireland, is situated in a courtyard behind number 20 lower Bridge Street. A traditional handpainted sign declares that the date of establishment was 1198. Certainly there was a tavern on this spot from mediaeval times. The only Liffey crossing before 1670 led directly into Bridge Street and this assured the inn of continuous patronage. The present building dates from 1668, subsequent to King Charles II's introduction of licensing laws.

The inn had all the trappings that we have come to associate with such establishments. The stable yards saw coaches, carriages and horsemen bustling to and fro, and grooms and serving wenches plying their way between the 43 bed chambers and the noisy ground floor tavern.

Many famous names down through the history of Dublin have been associated with the premises. Some were landed gentry, like the 17th century Sir Winston Churchill. Others had more than tankards of ale on their minds. Wolfe Tone, Oliver Bond (who lived just across the street) and Robert Emmet planned their risings here, only to be subsequently betrayed by treachery. The insurrectionists of 1916 and the figures of the War of Independence, including Michael Collins, gathered here.

In contrast to the ribaldry at the Brazen Head, Bridge Street itself was a rather religious place. The Capuchins established their first Irish house here in 1623. They were followed by the Dominicans in 1708 and later the Provincial Augustinians lived here. The Four Courts were also situated in Bridge Street for a time. The covered laneway into the Brazen Head was demolished in early 1984 and with it vanished some of the sense of antiquity one experienced when entering into it.

John's Lane, Thomas Street

In 1171, King Henry II, during a visit to Dublin, granted the lands around the present-day Thomas Street to the Victorine Canons. The citizens who settled in the district were to owe no allegiance to any local authority but only directly to the Crown. Thus the concept of a Liberty was born. The king named the main thoroughfare after Thomas À Beckett.

Shortly afterwards, in 1188, Ailred the Dane and his wife returned to Dublin after a pilgrimage to the Holy Land. Ailred, a wealthy land owner, carried palms on his way home and became known as Ailred le Palmer, Palmerstown is named after him. He was so impressed by the leper hospital of St John the Baptist in Jerusalem that he immediately set about building Ireland's first hospital on the site of the present Augustian Friary.

Ailred, his wife, and his subsequent followers, adopted the rule of St Augustine and in 1260 the hospital was handed over to the Augustinian Hospitallers — the order distinguished by a red cross on a white robe, the forerunner of the Red Cross symbol. Ailred and his followers are buried in the graveyard now occupied by Joseph Kelly & Son, Timber Merchants, across the road from the present church. The hospital and friary were suppressed in 1540 and for 230 years the friars worked by stealth. They used a stable in John's Lane to say Mass, until betrayed in 1717.

The present fine church of St John and St Augustine — colloquially called John's Lane — was built between 1862 and 1911. Designed by Pugin, the structure was funded by emigrant dollars and erected by men who were stone-masons by day and Fenians by night. Patrick Pearse's father, James (who was a Parnellite and an agnostic) carved the statues of the twelve apostles around the spire.

National College of Art and Design

The transfer of the National College of Art and Design (NCAD) from the inadequate Kildare Street location to the reconstructed Power's Distillery was both an inspired move and a remarkable achievement.

The distillery was originally an inn owned by James Power and it serviced the coaches travelling to the north and west. Suspecting that there might be a more lucrative future in the bottled spirit, Power converted his premises to a distillery in 1791. It joined the numerous other similar institutions in the district and when Powers finally closed in the mid 1970s it was the last operating distillery in the Liberties.

The largest structure, the granary, was totally gutted inside, leaving only the shell standing. Larger windows were discreetly built and new floors and roofs were constructed with only the huge old Baltic timber roof beams being retained. Glazed walks, corridors and conservatories were erected to offer improved communications within the complex. In some instances glass roofs highlight the rich iron framework while at the same time allowing for increased natural light.

The entrance arch to Joseph Kelly & Son

Tailors' Hall, Back Lane

From High Street we can see the rear of the old Tailors' Hall. The building, predating the Georgian renaissance, was built in 1706, during the reign of Queen Anne. Its only entrance is through an imposing archway (1714) leading off from the aptly named Back Lane. Tailors' Hall is the last remaining guild hall in Dublin.

A guild was a mediaeval form of craftsmen's trade union and the Guild of Tailors was inaugurated by Royal Charter in 1418. They commissioned this hall and subsequently shared it with the Guilds of Barbers, Tanners and some others.

In 1792, the Catholic Committee, led by Wolfe Tone, met here to debate and promote Catholic Emancipation. Their surreptitious gatherings gave the place the nickname the "Back Lane Parliament." The thick walls also overheard the conspiratorial whispers of Napper Tandy and the United Irishmen.

Down through the years the hall has been used as a Freemasons' Lodge and a dancing school. In 1968 Aer Lingus refurbished the building and opened it as a restaurant specialising in local food. Later the hall was used as a pub which staged folk sessions with a distinct Dublin flavour.

The hall lay virtually vacant from 1982 but in 1983 it became the headquarters of An Taisce, the National Trust for Ireland. Facilities will also be provided to the South Inner City Development Association and the Liberties Association. The building is owned by Dublin Corporation.

Opposite Tailors' Hall is the shoe factory of James Winstanley. Founded in Cornmarket in 1852 Winstanley moved to Back Lane in 1872. Archaeological digs in High Street revealed that shoe-making thrived here in the 12th century, so this firm carries on a great tradition. The Winstanleys are recorded in the registers of St Audoen's as far back as the 16th century and James Winstanley himself was elected Lord Mayor of Dublin in 1890, but died before exercising his office. Today, from the oldest shoe factory in Ireland the fifth generation descendants of the founder sell their wares as far apart as New York and Tokyo.

Castle Street

This street is one of the city's most ancient thoroughfares and, along with adjoining High Street, was the main avenue in mediaeval Dublin. Nestling under the shelter of the walls of Dublin Castle, it became an important commercial and administrative centre.

As early as 1281 the King's Exchange, which became the Royal Mint for a time, was founded here. Many officials connected with the castle came to live in Castle Street. For neighbours they had several famous taverns, ironmongers and government offices. In later years the street was renowned for its publishing houses and booksellers. The rising of 1641 was plotted here in Sir Phelim O'Neill's house, right under the noses of the castle authorities. Another famous resident was Sir James Ware. He was born in Castle Street in 1594 and spent his life and fortune collecting rare Irish manuscripts which are now known as the Clarendon Papers. In nearby Hoey's Court (now demolished), Jonathan Swift was born in 1667.

Dublin's last wooden cagework house (reminiscent of 18th-century Bristol or indeed Holland where the design reputedly originated) was removed in 1813 and stood on the site of the present-day shored-up boot and shoe repair shop of T. H. Barnwell.

In the firm founded by his father in 1881, Thomas Henry Barnwell still plies his trade in the oldest shoemaking business in the Liberties. A master shoemaker, he can vividly recall the days when the cobbled street echoed to the march of the British military. During the second World War his firm of 13 employees helped to provide the thousands of extra boots required by the Army.

A verse seen in the window of the shop:

We sole the living but not the dead
With the best of Leather, Wax and Thread
A good many patients have come to our Door
Worn out, run down and feeling "Foot Sore"
Though we use neither Poultice, Plastic or Pill,
We cure all sick Soles no matter how ill.

The combination finishing machine, which is over one hundred years old, works from a one and a half horse power motor and scours, burnishes, trims and polishes the leather.

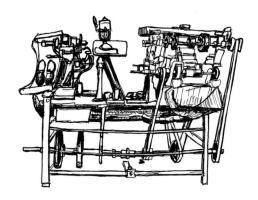

St Patrick's Cathedral

During a visit to Dublin St Patrick is reputed to have baptised some converts at a sacred well beside the River Poddle. A wooden church named after him was later erected at the spot and became one of the four main Celtic churches of pre-Danish Dublin. A 9th century stone slab which may have covered the well was excavated in 1901 and is on view inside the present-day cathedral.

Following the Anglo-Norman invasion, John Comyn was appointed in 1181 as Archbishop of Dublin by King Henry II. Comyn, not wishing to be subject to the jurisdiction of the city provosts or to be under the influence of the Priory of Christ Church, established his church on the site of St Patrick's, which was conveniently located outside the walls. He began to build his great stone church in 1191. The present building dates from 1225, although the baptistry may date from Comyn's time. St Patrick's became a cathedral in 1213 and the seat of Ireland's first university in 1320. It functioned as a university spasmodically until it was finally replaced by Trinity College in 1591. Jonathan Swift was Dean from 1713-45 during a time when one of Europe's worst slums encroached on all sides of the cathedral. The Huguenots had moved into the area to establish their weaving industry, and their unfortunate labourers, who worked for a pittance, were living with families fifteen or more to a single room.

The cathedral has suffered greatly from storms, fires, desecration, neglect and, more recently, from atmospheric pollution. The original tower was destroyed by fire in 1362 and had to be rebuilt, but the spire did not follow until 1750. Dublin's first public clock was erected on this tower in 1660. The existing building embodies the history and heritage of Ireland in a unique way. It embraces within its walls the principal traditions, religious and cultural, which have fashioned the fabric of Irish history. It is a visible witness to the need for reconciliation. The shades of Swift and Stella, Carolan and Philpot Curran, Ormond and Kildare -jointly associated with the famous door of reconciliation (1462) - the knights of the Order of St Patrick, King William and Schomberg, are all here together with many more.

The Guinness Family were mainly responsible for the saving of the church from total collapse. From the 1860s they spent a small fortune in restoring the fabric of the building and in preserving the interior. They cleared the slums from the north side in 1901 and laid out the beautiful park. Public subscription enabled further corrective work to be carried out in 1976. But more money still needs to be found.

It takes £100,000 per annum, which is £11.40 per hour, to maintain the Cathedral, and this figure does not include any major repairs or renovation. For example £35,000 was spent in 1984 in replacing part of the nave roof.

This conventional type of horse trough with protective bollards was to be found in many city streets and a few are still in evidence. St Patrick's Close is the home of the one below.

Marsh's Library

Dubliners have a tendency to take the city's worthwhile curiosities and historic institutions for granted. How many of us have bothered to interrupt our busy shopping and business schedules to view the Book of Kells or visit the National Library? Lamentations were heard from countless citizens who had always meant to climb the 166 steps of Nelson's Pillar before it was ignominiously blown up in 1966.

To my own shame I only recently made my first excursion to Marsh's Library, next door to St Patrick's Cathedral. Almost nothing has changed since the library was founded in 1701 by Archbishop Narcissus Marsh, a former Provost of Trinity College. Larger inside than you might first suspect, the library has a scholarly atmosphere, heavy with the scent of leather and age and disturbed only by the measured ticking of a hundred-year-old clock.

The ranks of dark oak bookcases, each with carved and lettered gables topped by a mitre, the heavy wooden shutters, old chairs and desks, framed pictures and feather-quilled pens all contribute to the prevading sense of quaintness and antiquity. At the far end of the building are the three famous wired alcoves or ''cages''.

Marsh's foundation was the first public library in Ireland and now ranks as one of the oldest in these islands. It was designed by Sir William Robinson who was also the architect of the Royal Hospital in Kilmainham. Marsh, who, among other activities, actively promoted the Irish language, paid £2,500 in 1705 for the 10,000-book collection of Edward Stillingfleet. There are now 25,000 books dating from the 15th to the 18th centuries covering subjects ranging from medicine, science and mathematics to music, travel, navigation and history.

The condition of the books is causing concern. However, a book restoration programme under the supervision of a distinguished rare books expert is in progress. The reader will appreciate that rare and valuable books need very special attention: otherwise, even more damage may be caused. This skilful work must all be done by hand and is both slow and very expensive.

Jonathan Swift was Governor of the Library for many years and some mementos from his term of office are on permanent display. The Library is administered by a Board of Governors and Guardians and is open to all visitors, including those who might just like to have a look around for a step back in time.

The American Irish Foundation has generously provided Marsh's with substantial funds for the restoration and development of the Library and for the repair and restoration of the books. This is especially welcome as the Library receives only one thousand pounds from the State per year. It does not receive any money from the Church of Ireland.

The entrance gate and front of Marsh's Library

Coombe Hospital Memorial

When developing a site in the Coombe for an enlightened housing scheme, Dublin Corporation decided to retain the portico of the old maternity hospital. The inscription on the plaque relates the following story:

"Towards the end of the year 1825, two women, whilst making a vain attempt to reach the Rotunda Hospital, perished together with their new born babies, in the snow. When it became known, a number of benevolent and well disposed persons founded the Coombe Lying-in Hospital in the year 1826 for the relief of poor lying-in women. Leading the charitable committee was a Mrs Margaret Boyle of Upper Baggot Street, Dublin.

The portico surrounding this plaque formed the entrance until the year 1967, when the hospital moved to a new location in Dolphin's Barn. It has been retained and restored by Dublin Corporation as a memorial to the many hundreds of mothers who gave birth to future citizens of Ireland in the Coombe Lying-in Hospital, and also to the generosity of the staff and friends of the Hospital."

On the six steps at the rear of the portico are inscribed 24 nicknames of some of the Coombe's most memorable eccentrics. The list was compiled by Éamonn MacThomáis, who has an encyclopaedic knowledge of the Liberties' lore. the names reveal typical Dublin wit and a capacity to be acidly descriptive. Read the roll call and let your imagination do the rest.

Hairy Yank, Stab the Rasher, Jembo no-Toes, Shell Shock Joe, The Magic Soap Man, The Grindstone Man, Johnny Wet Bread, Soodlum, The Prince of Denmark, Burgler Dunne, Johnny Forty Coats, Houdini, The Earl of Dalcashin, Windy Mills, Lady Hogan, The Tuggers, Rags Bottles and Bones, LoveJoy and Peace, The Umbrella Man, Hamlet, Damn the Weather, Dunlavin and Michael Bruen.

The Lord Mayor of the day, Alderman Fergus O'Brien, T.D., officially opened the housing scheme and the memorial on 20th November, 1980.

Portobello House, Grand Canal

The construction of the Grand Canal in 1772 was one of the great engineering feats in this country. It ran all the way from Dublin to the Shannon, and the rise and fall in the land meant that an intricate system of locks had to be constructed. Work commenced on the canal in 1756 and was only finally completed in 1804, when it was joined to the Shannon.

The Grand Canal, and its sister waterway, the Royal Canal, built some 25 years later by a man called Binns, were important means of transportation for goods, livestock and passengers. The Grand Canal Company, the operators of the south city canal, was comprised of many of the gentry of the day who saw it as a significant development in transport. Barges could carry the heavy tonnage which could not ordinarily be sent along unpaved roads.

Travel on the canals was also a leisurely, safe and comfortable way for passengers. It was quite upmarket and chic to take a barge and avoid the dusty or muddy, hole-ridden roads. To this end hotels were built along the route and the most lavish of these was at Portobello Bridge.

Opened in 1807, the Grand Canal Hotel, or "La Touche House" as it was once called, was a splendid building erected in the best traditions of the day. It was the passenger terminus for many years before eventually becoming a nursing home. Completely restored, it is now used for commercial offices. The harbour beside it is largely filled in.

In 1861, a horse-drawn bus plunged through the railings of Portobello bridge and all six passengers wre drowned. They included Michael Gunn, father of the founders of the Gaiety Theatre, and relatives of Daniel O'Connell.

Grand Canal Barges

In 1950, the Grand Canal was nationalised and control passed to C.I.E. The rapid decline in traffic after the war years forced the cessation of all commercial activity. The last barge left James's Street Harbour, carrying a load of Guinness porter to Limerick, on 27th May, 1960, thus ending a 156 year tradition.

In 1834 "Scotch" or "Fly" boats were introduced. These could carry 90 passengers and, because of their shallow draught, four horses at a gallop could pull them up to 10 m.p.h. They left Portobello Harbour at 7 a.m. and arrived in Tullamore by 4 p.m. Charles Bianconi and other coach operators provided overland connections at the various destinations en route. In 1846 over 120,000 passengers were carried. The advent of the railways finally eclipsed the canals and the last passenger boat left in 1853. Cargo, consisting of bricks, timber, grain, turf, etc., was still important and by the late 1860s steam tugs were introduced.

In 1911 the Canal Company pioneered diesel powered barges, the first in the British Isles, and soon most of the 200 or more boats operating on the system were motorised. Up till then it took a crew of three, working sixteen hours a day, four days to reach Limerick from Dublin.

The second World War brought a brief respite to the diminishing fortunes of the Grand Canal Company. The Government built 29 wooden horse-drawn barges and in this period over 200,000 tons of turf were transported to fuel-starved Dublin.

The barge (No. 93E) pictured at the Robert Emmet Bridge was originally horse-drawn and only motorised in 1928 by Vickers (Ireland). With the C.I.E. takeover it joined the Canal Engineering Department as a gravel-cum-maintenance craft. The yard in the background belongs to Gordon's Fuel Merchants, who themselves used to own four barges to carry turf to the city.

In 1983 the Office of Public Works took over the running of the canals from C.I.E.

Rathmines Town Hall

One of the most famous landmarks in Dublin is the clock tower of the old Rathmines Town Hall. Rathmines had its own independent Town Commissioners during the latter half of the 19th century and they administered a growing, self-contained urban area with a population of just under 30,000.

The commissioners appointed Sir Thomas Drew, the architect of many of the city's Victorian splendours, to build for them their new Town Hall which was to be made ready for their first meeting in their new and enhanced status as members of the Rathmines and Rathgar Urban District Council in January, 1899. The attractive clock reputedly cost £164-10s-0d and gained the dubious reputation of being a "four-faced liar", which I hope is no longer deserved. The clock still possesses its melodic chimes which ring out every quarter of an hour.

As well as being the administrative headquarters of the council, the Town Hall also became a very popular social centre. Concerts, dances, plays and meetings were held; Percy French performed here in 1899 and Marconi demonstrated his new wireless telegraphy invention. A pioneer Edison film was shown in the hall in 1902. During the War of Independence, due to its strategic position, British forces occupied the building. Local intervention and persuasion stopped them removing the splendid huge carved oak fireplace from the Council Chamber.

Much to the annoyance of the residents of Rathmines, 1930 saw the dissolution of the local District Council and its absorption into the Dublin City Borough. In the following year the Town Hall was leased from Dublin Corporation to accommodate the School of Domestic Economy. Twenty-seven years later it passed to the School of Management Studies. It is now the home of the Rathmines Senior College, part of the City of Dublin Vocational Education Committee.

The name Rathmines comes from the Irish *Rath Maoinis* or the Ring Fort of Moenes, an Anglo-Norman who was granted land here in 1279.

P. Liddy '84

Trinity House, Charleston Road, Ranelagh

Trinity House is a highly successful conversion from a disused Methodist Church to a modern office building. After surmounting incredible (and costly) planning difficulties, architect Reg Chandler of Chandler Lavin & Associates and Ambrose and John McInerney of McInerney Properties Ltd. tastefully converted this very interesting and ornate building.

Only essential external alterations were made and the ecclesiastical beauty of the interior was enhanced whenever possible. A modern "bubble" lift co-exists side by side with a reception desk fashioned from the carved pine pulpit. The third floor reveals the roof beams, trusses and cast-iron tie-bars in a way not appreciated in the original form.

The building was the overall winner in the Corporation's 1983 Cultural and Environmental Awards.

Montrose House, Donnybrook

Situated in the grounds of R.T.E., this Georgian mansion dates back to at least 1750. While its beginnings are a little sketchy, the house may have been remodelled or largely rebuilt in 1835. By 1837 the Jamesons, of distillery fame, lived there.

At this point an extraordinary and apt coincidence arises, which links the Jameson family with radio communications. Annie, the daughter of Andrew Jameson, married Giuseppe Marconi, whom she had met while studying in Bologna. Their son, Guglielmo, born in 1874, is credited with inventing wireless telegraphy for use by land stations and ships at sea. It is improbable that he visited Montrose, as the Jamesons had left a year before he arrived for his first visit to Ireland in 1892. So the story that Marconi conducted experiments in the house that was to be the future headquarters of our radio and television service is little more than a romantic fable.

The house passed to new owners in 1897 and, until 1947, when the National University bought the site, such illustrious people as Malcolm Inglis (Heiton's Coal), the Martin family (T. & C. Martin) and Major General Vincent Kelly, who fought in the Boer War, lived there.

Montrose House would have ended up in the campus of U.C.D. but for an unusual exchange. The land originally purchased by the Office of Public Works for R.T.E. divided the existing properties of the College so a deal was struck to swop it for the Montrose site.

The house is in magnificent condition today and the fine fireplaces, which were purchased for safekeeping by the Irish Georgian Society, have been replaced again in their rightful home. There are definite plans, as soon as finances permit, to house the Broadcasting Museum here. At present the museum is situated in Rathmines.

Thomas Prior House, Merrion Road

In 1792 The Masonic Order in Ireland established a charity to educate and maintain female children of deceased members, and the resultant schools were among some of the first in the country to offer separate teaching for girls. These schools were amalgamated under one roof when the Masonic Female Orphan School was opened in 1882. The design of the building was entrusted to the architectural firm of McCurdy and Mitchell. The foundation stone of the school was laid in 1880 by the then Grand Master, the Duke of Abercorn. Most of the building costs were funded from members' subscriptions and from the takings of a grand bazaar.

The institution was initially conducted as an orphanage, offering only a basic education, but, in time, more emphasis was placed on the academic side. A contemporary quotation assures us that the girls were "carefully sheltered from the trials and temptations of life."

A decision was taken in 1972 to sponsor children in schools of their parents' choice, and the premises were duly sold to the Royal Dublin Society who renamed it Thomas Prior House. Prior, a friend of Dean Swift, was a founder member of the Dublin Society and its first secretary. But for his indefatigable support and deep sense of practical patriotism the society might not have survived its growing pains. He died in 1751, and a monument, carved by Van Nost, was erected to his memory in Christ Church Cathedral.

Under the auspices of the R.D.S. Science Committee this building is now used for youth science activities, and as a centre for the publication of works on the history of scientific development in Ireland. Other occupiers include the School of Irish Studies, the Royal Horticultural Society of Ireland, the Crafts Council and the Hereford Breeders Society.

Prior House still preserves links with its Masonic past. Windows and stone carvings proclaim the Order's symbols including the Stars of David and Solomon and the sign of the Compass and Rule, the tools of the operative mason.

American Embassy, Ballsbridge

In 1956 the Government of the United States of America bought the old offices of the Irish Tourist Board at the corner of Elgin and Pembroke Roads in Ballsbridge. The original houses were demolished and by May 1964 the new Embassy building was completed.

At the time it was hailed as an architectural triumph and won accolades from all sides. An Taisce, the National Trust of Ireland, honoured the Embassy with its premier award: ''For effective development of a prominent corner site on a main city approach, for sympathy of scale with existing environment and interest of character, without imitation of surrounding buildings and for integration with existing trees and street setting.'' The design has worn extremely well and is as futuristic today as it was 20 years ago, but the architects, American, John MacL. Johansen and Irishman, Michael Scott, looked as much to fifth century Celtic traditions as to daring new concepts. The resultant merging of styles was meant to express the close relationship between the United States and Ireland.

The rotunda form of the building, inviting and attractive from any angle, is surrounded by a ''moat'' of flowering shrubbery which is bridged at the entrances. Inside there is an impressive atrium flooded by natural lighting and encompassed by a repeat of the modular unit pattern of the exterior which fronts the balconies for the offices on all three floors. Mostly Irish materials were used for the building which was constructed by G. & T. Crampton. The base is Irish granite and the terrazzo floors are of Connemara marble.

The Embassy is staffed by about 40 Irish and 30 Americans including a detachment of six armed Marine Guards. The eight departments, Administration, Agriculture, Consular, Economic/Commercial, Military Liaison, Political, Public Affairs and Security are all under the direction of the Ambassador who is usually not a career diplomatic but a political appointee of the President.

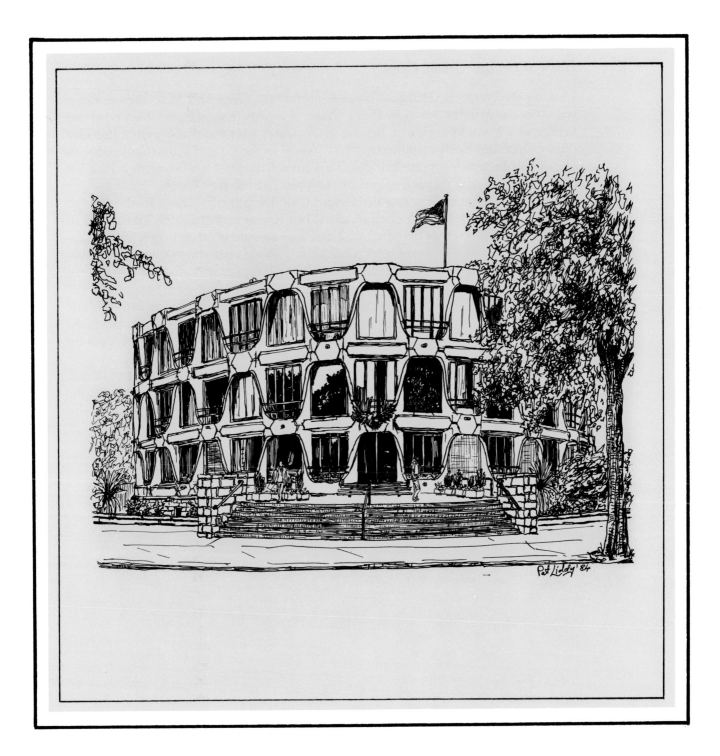

Huband Bridge, Grand Canal

Linking the terraced Georgian houses of Herbert Place and Warrington Place with those across the canal in Percy Place is a picturesque hump-backed stone bridge which would appear to belong in a country backwater more than in a city centre. Huband Bridge, named after a director in the Grand Canal Company, is one of Dublin's oldest stone bridges. This stretch of canal is a favourite haunt for artists and was also much beloved by the poet Patrick Kavanagh.

The first bridge built across the Grand Canal was the so-called Rialto Bridge (named after the famous Venetian span) but it was unfortunately destroyed in 1939. From when it was first erected it became a popular attraction with Sunday excursionists whose custom and pastime it was to visit the burgeoning city's newly-erected structures. During 1791 several more attractive bridges were added, including the Huband.

The view from Huband Bridge opens from upper Mount Street into Mount Street Crescent where, in the centre island, stands the graceful shape of St Stephen's Church. This was the last building in Dublin to be commissioned by the Church of Ireland on purely classical lines.

It was designed by John Bowden and built in 1824. An unusual feature is that the unornamented sides and rear are fully exposed and not concealed by neighbouring buildings, an aspect which in no way detracts from the grandeur of the church.

P.LIDDY '83

Number 1, Merrion Square

Number 1, Merrion Square is a well-known city landmark, notable not least for the somewhat out-of-character addition to its gable end. This side of Merrion Square was completed by 1764 to the designs of John Ensor, who was commissioned for the purpose by Viscount Fitzwilliam. The houses were extremely well planned and proportioned and the square itself was second only in size to St Stephen's Green.

I am not certain as to the date when the Victorian-style extension was built on to Number 1, but it seems to have existed when the Wildes occupied the house from 1855 to 1876. Sir William Wilde was growing in eminence as a physician when he decided to move from 21 Westland Row (where his son, Oscar, was born) to the more fashionable Merrion Square.

Sir William was held in very high esteem by his peers, but unfortunately involved himself in a relationship with a nineteen-year-old servant girl, Moll Travers. When he refused to divorce Lady Wilde and marry her, Moll harassed her lover and eventually brought a famous libel case against him. She was awarded one farthing, but Sir William lost £2,000 in legal costs. Lady Jane Wilde (known as Speranza) was a poetess of some distinction and her literary circle of friends must have influenced and encouraged her son, Oscar.

Today, like most of the other buildings around the square, the house contains a number of offices.

To the left of the drawing, at the end of Lower Merrion Street, is the dark front of Merrion Hall, where a non-denominational Christian Assembly worships. The hall was built in 1863 and the interior, with its fine two-tiered balconies, was designed to accommodate 2,500 people.

The Bailey, Duke Street

The pub has the original door of 7, Eccles Street, complete with Egyptian-head knocker and weather board. The following text, which appears beside the door, explains all.

"This is the door of Number 7, Eccles Street, Dublin, immortalised by James Joyce as the home of Leopold Bloom in *Ulysses*! Bloom is the hero of the book and his home had a special significance for Joyce. When discussing *Ulysses* with his friends he always referred to it as 'The Blue Book of Eccles'.

The house, in fact, was the home of his friend John Francis Byrne who was to become 'Crawley', Stephen's companion in a *Portrait of an Artist as a Young Man*. The final part of *Ulysses,* the 'Penelope' sequence, Molly Bloom's famous soliloquy, takes place at Number 7.

When the house itself was demolished in April 1967, the door was bought by John Ryan, then owner of the Bailey. He installed it on the premises and on 16th June, 1967, it was unveiled by the poet Patrick Kavanagh."

P. Liddy '83

Clare Street

Clare Street was named after John Fitzgibbon, the unpopular Earl of Clare, who was Attorney-General in 1783 and was later to become Lord Chancellor and Speaker of the Irish House of Lords. This short street, leading from the environs of Trinity College, opens out into the majestic sweep of Merrion Square.

The street is mainly famous for the Mont Clare Hotel and for the quaint old premises of Greene's, the new and second-hand booksellers.

Founded in 1843 by the Greene family, it passed to the Quinns in 1892. It was subsequently acquired in 1912 by Hubert Pembrey who in 1916/17 added the canopy and converted the upstairs living quarters to extend the size of the premises. Herbert Pembrey's son Herbert is the postmaster in the sub-post office attached to the shop, in turn Herbert's sons Eric and Vivian run the book business. David, the most recent member of the family to join the firm, represents the fourth generation.

The shop has always been a Mecca for hunters of second-hand books, including schoolbooks and those of Irish interest. This section of the book business is still booming. Until 1958, Greene's was also a public lending library. Famous authors who once browsed among the stalls and shelves included the Yeats brothers, Frank O'Connor, Patrick Kavanagh and, more recently Mary Lavin and Anthony Cronin.

Next to Greene's and fronting on to Merrion Square West is the Apothecaries Hall. Established in 1791 by an Act of the Irish Parliament, the Apothecaries Company was already one of the old Guilds of Dublin. The Apothecaries were the forerunners of today's medical fraternity and, until quite recently, members of the Company sat for recognised examinations to admit them to various medical qualifications.

Rutland Memorial Fountain, Merrion Square

Two hundred years ago an atrociously inadequate city water supply, delivered along old wooden pipes, aggravated the almost intolerable living conditions of the poor. Because of the lack of personal hygiene facilities thousands died from the series of fevers which swept Dublin during the 18th century.

The popular Duke of Rutland, who became Viceroy in 1785, lived his young life to the full until he succumbed to a fever at the age of 33. He had embellished the Viceregal Lodge (now Áras an Uachtaráin) with a fine collection of paintings and his patronage of the arts and the social scene was renowned.

Rutland Square (now Parnell Square) was named after him to honour the memory of his frequent visits to the Rotunda Gardens and the Assembly Rooms. It was also decided to erect a monument that would be classical in style and yet useful to the poor of Dublin. In 1791 the Duke of Rutland Memorial Fountain, with its twin water jets, was built and opened to the public. Designed by Henry Aaron Baker, a protégé of Gandon, it is finely embellished with stone urns and medallions.

Now disused, the fountain had become a victim of sad neglect until refurbished in 1975.

Leinster House Gates

Deposed T.D.s and various protesting groups probably fail to cast admiring glances at these wrought iron masterpieces as they are politely closed against them, but it is only when the gates are shut that their intricate ornamentation can be fully appreciated. Standing over 18 feet high, they display a rich tapestry of decorative designs surmounted overall by the Brian Boru harp.

They were built at the turn of the century for the then owners of Leinster House, the Royal Dublin Society, by the Art Iron and Brass Works of J. & C. McGloughlin Ltd.

It was very fashionable during the Victorian era for institutions and individuals to commission fine gates and railings. The blacksmiths were either supplied with detailed plans by their clients or were given only an outline idea from which they imaginatively and skilfully created the working drawings.

Low wages in those days kept the prices within affordable limits. In 1907, the craftsmen smiths in McGloughlins only earned 38 shillings for a backbreaking 51½-hour week. Today's labour costs, assuming their skills could still be found, would make similar style gates prohibitively expensive.

J. & C. McGloughlin was founded in Cuffe Lane by a returned emigrant, John McGloughlin, in 1875. After the firm moved to South Great Brunswick Street (Pearse Street) his sons, John and Charles, took over and set up a limited company in 1896.

Lamp from the grounds of Leinster House with a modern (1984) counterpart alongside the new security railings.

P. LIDDY '84

Leinster House

When the building of Leinster House (then known as Kildare House) commenced in 1745, people wagged their heads and doubted the wisdom of the chosen site. It was, after all, being erected in a desolate area far removed from the city's fashionable quarters. However, Lord Kildare, the future Duke of Leinster and father of Lord Edward Fitzgerald, knew well his own mind and correctly predicted that fashion would follow him across the Liffey.

Richard Cassels was the architect of this ambitious project, which was to be the largest private mansion built in the city. Lord Kildare and Cassels could not agree whether the house was a city or a country residence so a compromise was agreed. The Kildare Street facade would be the city entrance and the Merrion Square side would present the country house image. Officially, therefore, the building has two fronts and no rear. James Hoban's design of the White House in Washington, before it was burned down in 1812, is said to have been modelled on Leinster House.

When the Fitzgeralds fell on hard times they sold the property in 1815 to the Dublin Society (later to become the Royal Dublin Society). The Society established a library, gallery and museum, the forerunners of the National Gallery, the National Library and the Natural History and National Museums. Leinster Lawn, the expansive sward in front of the Merrion Square entrance (shown in the drawing) was the location for the Society's first agricultural show in 1830. Subsequent Spring and Horse Shows were also held here.

Royalty also visited the Lawn, King George IV in 1821 and Victoria and Albert attended William Dargan's Exhibition, with its steel and glass domes rivalling the Crystal Palace in London, in 1853.

In 1922, the Government of the Irish Free State virtually commandeered Leinster House, giving £68,000 to the R.D.S. as compensation. The Dáil Chamber was in fact the Society's theatre which was ultra-modern for its day. It was the first theatre in Ireland to be lit by electricity and also boasted probably the first demonstration of cinematographic projection in this country.

The obelisk in the lawn commemorates Michael Collins, Arthur Griffith and Kevin O'Higgins and was erected in 1950. It is 65 feet high and is surmounted by a gilt bronze flame. The flame and bronze reliefs at the base were the work of Laurence Campbell R.H.A., the inscriptions are in letterings designed by Colm Ó Lochlainn and the scheme was carried out under the direction of Mr Raymond McGrath, principal architect of the Office of Public Works.

Royal Hibernian Hotel, Dawson Street

The Royal Hibernian Hotel first opened for business in 1751 and, apart from the Brazen Head Inn, was Dublin's oldest. Business was brisk from the foundation but its normal routine was temporarily interrupted by the rising of 1798. General Humbert and his captured fellow French officers were held in Andrew Falkner's Mail Coach office at No. 12 Dawson Street — now the head office of New Ireland Assurance Co.

In the early part of the 19th century, Charles Bianconi set up a major staging post for his countrywide coaching service at the Hibernian. By 1843, the Royal Mail coaches departed from the Hibernian to Sligo, Limerick, Mullingar, Galway, Athlone, Monaghan and other towns. The Duke Lane entrance led to the stables and the forge.

At the turn of the century, the hotel was the epitome of Victorian high life. It featured daily band recitals in the music room, and a winter garden with fountains. It had smoking, reading, writing and tea rooms, and the new sanitation was installed. The cost of a private bedroom there was three shillings and dinner cost two shillings.

The doors of the hotel were finally closed on 11th February, 1984. On the closing night the hotel was packed with nostalgic revellers. There were scuffles as crowds tried to gain entry. Souvenir hunters disappeared with crockery and removable decorations. When the hotel was finally demolished in September 1984 – only the ornate ceiling of the Staircase Hall was saved – Dubliners felt a sense of loss for an old friend.

The old-world ambience of Mitchell's shop front in Kildare Street is illustrated below.

Mansion House

The Mansion House was originally built in 1705 for Joshua Dawson who was the developer of Dawson Street and Nassau Street. Dawson's town house, partly unfinished and seldom lived in, was sold to the Corporation in 1715 for £3,500. The Lord Mayor of the day took up residence and thus Dublin preceded the City of London by some 15 years in providing an official house for its Mayor.

Dublin has had a civic government since 1172, and the office of Mayor was instituted by Henry II in 1229 to act as a form of city magistrate. Sir Daniel Bellingham became the first Lord Mayor in 1665, and in 1841 Daniel O'Connell became the first Catholic elected to the office since the Reformation.

The house was originally faced in brick but was later plastered and the City coat of arms, the pediment and the canopy (1896) were added. The symbolic meaning of the 400-year-old coat of arms is somewhat obscure. The three castles may represent three of the city's old gates, or may be representations of Dublin Castle or city perimeter strongholds. The motto ''Obedientia Civium Urbis Felicitas'' translates as ''The obedience of the citizens produces a happy city''.

The imposing gates (shown here) lead through a graceful passageway to the Round and Meeting Rooms, where the first Dáil met in 1919. The Round Room was originally built to host George IV when he visited Dublin in 1821.

In the well-kept garden, a soothing fountain plays. The basin of the fountain was once inhabited by colourful goldfish, but these fell victims to vandals. Occasionally a baby fish may suddenly arrive, as the fountain water is supplied by the Grand Canal! The garden is also the annual breeding ground for one intrepid duck from Stephen's Green. It is on record that, on one occasion, she and her young entourage stopped the traffic during their procession back to the Green.

Mansion House Gates, manufactured in 1929.

114

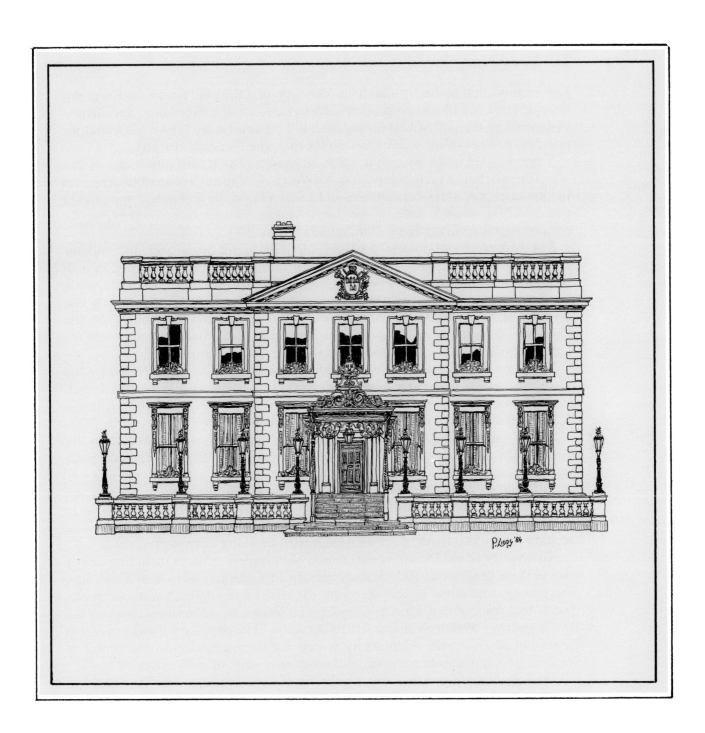

The Lord Mayor's Coach

Determined not to be upstaged by the city of London, which had recently provided its Lord Mayor with a resplendent carriage, the Aldermen, Sheriffs and Commons of the city of Dublin appointed a committee in 1763 to examine the possibility of providing a State Coach for their own leading citizen.

The original budget was set at £400, but years of procrastination meant that when the coach finally rumbled out of Mr William Whitton's coach-building firm in Dominick Street the cost had risen to £2,690.13s.5d. Its first public appearance was in 1791, when it carried the Lord Mayor, Henry Gore Sankey, to the celebrations honouring King William's birthday.

The exquisite workmanship of the carriage found wide acclaim, and the English Monarch's State Coach, built in Dublin in 1808, was modelled on it. It was eventually retired after the Eucharistic Congress in 1932. In 1975 Dublin Corporation decided to revamp the coach. The main restoration work was lovingly and magnificently carried out by the mechanical section of Dublin Corporation, who were assisted by a retired C.I.E. coach trimmer for the upholstery, and by the National Gallery for the painted panels.

The State Coach made its reappearance on St Patrick's Day 1976, and it has since participated in the annual parade each year and, on other formal occasions, such as when it carried the Lord Mayors of Dublin, Cork and Belfast to the R.D.S. on Aga Khan Cup day a couple of years ago.

Before each outing the wheels have to be removed and soaked in water overnight to make them swell a little and thus ensure that the metal tyres remain tightly fixed.

Although designed for six horses, it is currently pulled by a team of four, supplied by Mr Joe McGrath from the Curragh. It is extremely difficult today to get trained teams such as this, and, were it not for Mr McGrath, it is doubtful if we would ever see this work of art on wheels trundle along our street again.

No drawing of old Dublin streets would be complete without including one or two of these ubiquitous 19th century cabs or broughams. They lasted well into this century and could be still seen into the 1940s and 1950s. A number of city hotels and commercial firms sponsored a collection of these broughams in the 1970s and they were seen on our streets yet again. The practice fell away in recent years but you can still occasionally see one of these vehicles in attendance at weddings. A fair number remain in the hands of private individuals.

The brougham illustrated was, like many of its peers, built in Ireland and was not a street cab as such but a private carriage. Contact to the driver was made by a bell.

Shelbourne Hotel, St Stephen's Green

Lord Shelburne's former town mansion was leased to the military from 1798 until 1818 when it was accidentally burnt down by a careless soldier. The owner, Henry White, built three Georgian houses on the cleared site. Unfortunately, a property slump followed the Act of Union and White was unable to find any residential buyers. After considerable hesitation he reluctantly let the houses to Martin Burke, whose plans to open an hotel filled White with apprehension in case the tone of the elegant square was diminished. As a result, his lease had some unusual conditions, including the stipulation that Burke retain the three separate entrances and not outwardly unify the buildings. Initially called Burke's Hotel, the name was soon changed to the Shelbourne and business flourished.

Burke died in 1863 and the premises were sold to hoteliers Jury, Cotton and Goodman. First purchasing the two houses next door, they pulled down the entire block and erected the present structure in 1867.

300 men worked alternate shifts from 4 a.m. to 9 p.m. and completed the hotel in only 10 months. The cost was £80,000. The equipment and furnishings were very modern for the time, there were even rooms for invalid guests. A quaint quote from *The Irish Builder* of 1867 proclaims that "the fire escape is capable of holding 30 persons at a time and the approach to it is most sensibly arranged from two stacks of water closets, the bottom sash of each being hinged giving easy access to it. In these water-closets are hung instructions for using the escape, that those who sit may read"!

Designed by John McCurdy, it is a magnificent building with the facade equally as sumptuous as the interior. The glazed porch, protecting guests from the weather, is a later addition and, flanking it, are four Egyptianesque statues, representing two Nubian princesses and their slave girls with shackles. The four bronze statues were cast in the studio of M.M. Barbezet of Paris. They originally held gas lamps.

The adjoining pair of Georgian houses are also part of the hotel. Number 32 was Lord de Montalt's mansion and possesses several fine ceilings. The large arched doorway next to the main building was built to allow access for de Montalt's carts, carrying produce from his country estates.

In a vast £4½ million refurbishing programme, the majority of the bedrooms and function rooms (the Irish Free State Constitution was drafted in function room 112 in 1922) have been tastefully restored and redecorated in complete harmony with their mid-Victorian surroundings. The foyer will soon be reconstituted to its former glory, and a major facelift is being carried out to the facade this year.

P. LIDDY '82

119

The establishment in 1831 of the Office of Public Works (O.P.W.) in effect nationalised the fragmented local public works boards scattered around the country. Commonly called the Board of Works, the organisation is directed by a Board of Commissioners who are responsible to the Minister of State at the Department of Finance.

During the great famines of 1845/6 and 1879 the Board rose to the awesome task of providing relief in the form of public work for over one million labourers.

After the calamities of 1916-23, the Commissioners had the daunting task of rebuilding many of the country's destroyed public buildings, including Dublin's Custom House, the G.P.O. and the Four Courts. The newly-formed Garda Síochána immediately required 837 stations and, of the 770 vacated by the R.I.C., 581 had been blasted apart or severely damaged. Later the O.P.W. designed and built Ireland's two main airports at Shannon (1936) and Dublin (1937).

Today, the Commissioners are responsible nationwide for the maintenance or building of government and public buildings, Garda and military establishments, post offices and telephone exchanges, national schools, waterways and harbours, prisons and ancient monuments and memorials. Also under their care are bridges, arterial drainage, parks and our embassies abroad.

In Dublin, the O.P.W. portfolio includes all the State buildings, the Phoenix Park and St Stephen's Green, the restoration of the Royal Hospital in Kilmainham and the Casino in Marino, St Enda's in Rathfarnham, the buildings in the Botanic Gardens and many of the public statues and memorials scattered around the city.

The headquarters of the O.P.W. occupies the former residence of the Monck family. Built in 1760 on the side of the Green known then as Monck's Walk, the building eventually passed to various owners, including a Lord Chancellor, until the Government purchased it in 1848. It was then converted into a Museum of Irish Industry and the two side wings were added, replacing two wooden gates leading to the back yards. Forty examples of Irish marble from Kilkenny, Cork and Galway can still be seen displayed in the entrance hall. The O.P.W. took over the premises in 1913.

The Commissioners maintain the fine traditions of their predecessors and, without the skills of the O.P.W. staff, an enormous amount of our national heritage would have been irredeemably lost.

Iveagh House, St Stephen's Green

Dr Robert Clayton, the Protestant Bishop of Cork and Ross, was an ambitious man, and eagerly sought the limelight of Dublin and its influential society. To this end he had a splendid town mansion built in 1736, so that he could be present during the so-called Dublin season, when the rich, the powerful and the nobility gathered for the parliamentary sessions. The site had cost £250. The building was the first house to be built in the city by the German, Richard Cassels, the architect of Leinster House.

Dr Clayton fell into disgrace when he publicly disputed aspects of the doctrine of the Trinity and eventually became mentally unhinged. He died in 1758 and is buried in the old graveyard in Donnybrook. His house was purchased from his widow by the Earl of Mountcashel and, in 1809, John Philpot Curran, Master of the Rolls, became the new owner. Curran was the father of Sarah, the fiancée of the ill-fated Robert Emmet. The original portico had, by 1793, been removed because of persistent thefts of the lead from the flat roof.

After Curran's death the house passed through a succession of barrister owners until Benjamin Lee Guinness bought it in 1856. Number 81 next door was soon acquired, and in 1866 the two buildings were joined and refaced in Portland stone to present the view familiar today. The house was further decorated and in 1896 the lavish ballroom was added to the rear.

Three generations of the Guinness family lived here until Rupert, second Earl of Iveagh (the title comes from Iveagh, Co Down), presented the house to the Irish nation in 1939. Since then it has been the headquarters of the Department of Foreign Affairs.

Newman House is named after Dr John Henry (later Cardinal) Newman, a native of London and first rector of the Catholic University. The block comprises number 86 next to the church and number 85, formerly known as Clanwilliam House. The latter was the earliest building on the south side of the Green. It was built by Richard Cassels in 1738 and it contains some of the finest plasterwork of the Francini brothers.

Number 86 was built in 1765 for Richard Chapell Whaley (the father of the notorious gambler Buck Whaley) and he had the stucco work executed by Robert West in a style to rival the Francinis. Richard's son, John, lived here until his death in 1847, when Charles Bianconi purchased the house on behalf of the Catholic University committee and Cardinal Cullen. Newman bought Clanwilliam House from Nicholas Ball, the first Catholic judge appointed after the relaxation of the Penal Laws. The two houses were combined and the Catholic University became a reality when the schools of Philosophy and Letters commenced in 1854.

The crouching lion over the main entrance - made of lead and not stone, as one might have supposed - has gazed down on the comings and goings of such notable figures as James Joyce, Francis Sheehy Skeffington and Gerard Manley Hopkins.

Today, the buildings, extensively restored after the University moved to Earlsfort Terrace in 1918, are used for student meetings, social clubs, examinations and seminars. The fine interiors deserve much more widespread appreciation.

The neo-Byzantine Collegiate Church of SS. Peter and Paul, commonly called University Church, opened in 1856. It was built on the remaining gardens of Clanwilliam House, hence the narrow entrance. A one-time Governor-General of India, John Hungerford Pollen, was the architect.

The interior is a rich tapestry in Irish marble quarried from Connemara, Galway, Armagh, Offaly and Kilkenny and, in style, is unlike any other church in Ireland. It is said to have influenced the design of the Catholic Westminster Cathedral. The original bell from the curiously suspended belfry is now kept in the Administration Block of U.C.D., Belfield, thus linking the new campus with its roots.

The inscription on the St Stephen's Green fountain announces: "Presented to the Corporation and the citizens of Dublin by Lady Laura Grattan 1880."

125

Fusiliers' Arch, St Stephen's Green

By the mid 19th century St Stephen's Green, much to the resentment of Dubliners, had become a private park accessible only to key holders. Sir Arthur Guinness, later to be named Lord Ardilaun, paid off the accrued debts of the park and arranged for an Act of Parliament to restore it to public use in 1877. Ownership passed to the Commissioners of Public Works who are still in charge today.

On a point of interest, Lord Ardilaun also left us the legacy of St Anne's Park in Clontarf, which had been his Dublin residence.

The Green, a quarter of a mile long on each side, can trace its origins back to mediaeval times when its overall area was somewhat larger. It was named after the Church of Saint Stephen, a chapel attached to the leper hospital which stood on the site of the present Mercers Hospital. Citizens used to use this open marshy space with Hoggen Green (College Green) to graze their livestock.

By 1664 the Corporation walled off about 27 acres and sold the remaining 33 acres in 90 building lots. Straight formal gravelled walks lined with elms and limes were laid and the park became a fashionable place to walk and be seen. Strollers could review parades of the yeomanry or even attend fireworks displays.

Unfortunately by the early 1800s the condition of the park had deteriorated and new walks were laid and trees replaced. The railings were erected and the outside walk was separated from the road by granite bollards linked by chains. The bollards and railings still survive. The landscaping subsequently carried out by Lord Ardilaun shaped the character of the park as it is today.

St Stephen's Green contains 14 commemorative monuments, the largest of which is the Fusiliers' Arch shown in the drawing. Built in 1907, it is a memorial to the officers and men of the Royal Dublin Fusiliers who lost their lives in the Boer War of 1899-1900. Their names are inscribed on the panels of the arch over the gates.

Some interesting shopfronts a short walk away in Dawson Street.

P. LIDDY '82

The Gaiety Theatre, South King Street

The continuing frenzy for demolishing complete blocks of Dublin's streets once more affords us the dubious advantage of viewing a familiar landmark from a new perspective. The full facade of the Gaiety Theatre can now be appreciated following the destruction of the south side of South King Street.

In 1871, the brothers John and Michael Gunn erected, in a mere 28 weeks, a magnificent palace for the performing arts. From the outset it differed from tis main rivals, The Royal, The Queens and Dan Lowry's (now the Olympia) in that it had no resident company, preferring instead to invite visiting companies to perform drama, musical comedy and opera.

The first performance to open in the Gaiety, on 27th November, 1871, was Oliver Goldsmith's *She Stoops to Conquer*. The first pantomine followed in December 1873. Two years later the famous D'Oyly Carte Company brought light opera to the stage. George Bernard Shaw had his first major Gaiety performance in 1907. In the mid 1920s the Rathmines and Rathgar Musical Society reached the high standards that we have now come to expect from this amateur group.

The Elliman family bought the Theatre in 1936 and the legendary partnership of Harry O'Donovan and Jimmy O'Dea ("Biddy Mulligan") was introduced a year later. No visiting companies could come during the war years so the Dublin Grand Opera Society was founded in 1941 to present opera in the theatre. In the early 1950s, the present Queen of the Theatre, Maureen Potter, teamed up with Jimmy O'Dea to form a duo that brought happiness and laughter to tens of thousands of young and young-at-heart alike.

The interior was built in the best traditions of the Victorian theatre and the recent refurbishing has revealed not only the richness of the decor but has enhanced its beauty and improved the facilities beyond anything the Gunn brothers ever imagined. No modern structure could ever contain what the words of the late Michael Mac Liammoir described as the "ghosts in the gilded shadows."

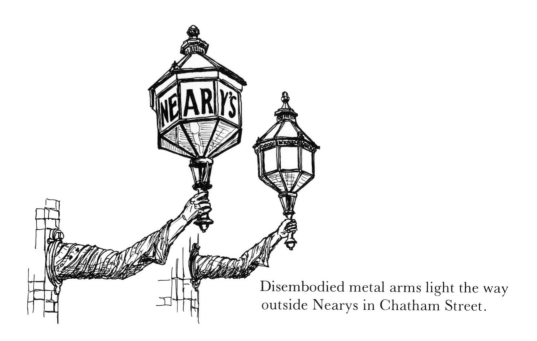

Disembodied metal arms light the way outside Nearys in Chatham Street.

Civic Museum, South William Street

Not as well known as it deserves, this building houses an important collection of exhibits associated with the history of Dublin. Old photographs, Malton prints (presented by President Seán T. O'Kelly for the opening of the Museum in 1953), maps and other documents record the various highlights in the development of the city.

Nostalgic items of street furniture ranging from old bridge name tablets and pavement coal-hole covers to the pitted head of Horatio Nelson, salvaged from the bomb-blasted ruins of the Pillar, are prominently displayed.

The building was originally erected for the Society of Artists and their first exhibition took place here in 1766. They were followed in 1791 by the Corporation, which had just vacated the crumbling Tholsel. The Corporation used the exhibition room for its meetings until 1852, when it moved to the City Exchange on Cork Hill.

Coachman
In 1888 Thomas Sexton M.P., Lord Mayor, designed and produced a uniform for his coachman at his own expense. It was made by Robert Sexton & Sons of 50 Dawson Street, a firm established since 1853. This fully outfitted model and a complete description are on view in the Civic Museum.

The Court of Conscience, a Mayoral tribunal for settling petty debts and trade disputes, met here from 1811 to 1924. Their room, with its courtroom-like furnishings, was used by the outlawed Supreme Court of the Irish Republic from 1920 to 1922.

The Municipal College of Music started in this building before moving to Chatham Row. Dublin's first horse-drawn fire brigade was also located here for a time. The Guild of Merchants met in the house from 1810 to 1823 and that august body of students, the Trinity College Historical Society, debated the serious issues of the day here when it was banned from within the College walls during 1794.

Today, the Civic Museum (also known as the City Assembly House) is still owned by the Corporation and is managed by the Old Dublin Society, who meet here for lectures on aspects of old Dublin or Dubliners in the winter season.

P. Liddy '83

Clarendon Street

Clarendon Street was laid out in 1685 by William Williams (who named William Street after himself). A narrow, undistinguished thoroughfare, it eventually evolved into an area of small business and craft shops. There were glass blowers, tailors, pawnbrokers, silversmiths, roof slaters, grocers, horse dealers, dairymen and even a muffin and crumpet shop.

By the end of the 18th century the houses on the street were degenerating into tenements. The locality soon gained a reputation for its brothels, which was in stark contrast to nearby fashionable Grafton Street. Johnston's Court contained small shops, tenements and cottages, where nailers plied their trade. Whole families young and old were involved in the noisy and smoky business of forging and shaping nails.

A very early and famous school of The Holy Faith Sisters stood in Clarendon Street but it is now demolished. The clergy of nearby St Teresa's had to live and work among the scenes of destitution, cheap labour and bawdiness for many years. The Discalced Carmelites founded their church in 1793 while the Penal Laws were still in force, and they hid the structure behind the tenements. In later years the church was extended to its present size. Altar boys who served here included Kevin Barry, Seán Lemass and Noel Purcell. Nearby St Teresa's Hall was the first home of the Abbey Players.

In what is now a small enclosed car park (to the extreme right of the drawing) was the old stable yard of the cab driver James Fitzharris. Known as "Skin the Goat", Fitzharris drove the Invincibles from the Phoenix Park after they had murdered Cavendish and Burke in 1882.

Across the street is the splendid new Powerscourt Townhouse Centre which has done much to enliven the district with its myriad of specialised shops and restaurants. The development, by Cork-based Power Securities, comprises Powerscourt House (1774) on the William Street side and the old offices of the Commissioners of Stamp Duties (designed by Francis Johnston, architect of the G.P.O.) which were built on three sides around the courtyard at the back of the mansion. The courtyard has now been attractively roofed over and the whole concept has been tastefully executed much on the lines of the refurbished Covent Garden in London.

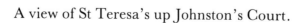

A view of St Teresa's up Johnston's Court.

POWERSCOURT TOWNHOUSE CENTRE

P.Liddy '84

Grafton Street

Grafton Street has a unique atmosphere. The street, now the most fashionable shopping precinct in the city, had very humble beginnings. When the main axis of the city stretched from Essex Bridge past Dublin Castle to Trinity College, it was only a narrow laneway linking Hoggen Green (now College Green) with St Stephen's Green. However, with the building of Carlisle Bridge (O'Connell Bridge), the axis switched to connect the Rotunda on Rutland (Parnell) Square to St Stephen's Green.

This lead to the building of Kildare, Dawson and Grafton Streets. Grafton Street itself started as a quiet residential area but soon turned into a street of shops, academies and institutions. The street was one of the first to be lit by electricity.

Traffic has always been somewhat of a hazard in this busy, narrow and winding thoroughfare. After long debate it has finally been pedestrianised. This has led to a plethora of street artists performing their acts to passersby. The street is again full of wonder and magic.

Bewley's Cafe, Grafton Street

Bewley's Cafes have been a popular meeting place for generations of citizens and visitors, who come to sample the renowned sticky buns, barm bracks and assorted confectioneries, washed down with freshly roasted coffee, exotic teas or Jersey milk supplied from the firm's own herd in Co Kildare.

The cafes maintain a turn-of-the-century ambience by their retention of solid mahogany counters and panelling, high ceilings, interesting nooks and corners, and even the old wooden chairs. Inside the window, the venerable old Probat machine gently whisks and roasts the coffee beans.

In the early 1840s, Joshua Bewley arrived from England and opened his small tea and coffee shop in Sycamore Alley, beside the Olympia. In due course the first of the three famous city centre shops, 13 South Great George's Street, was opened. Initially coffee was only sold in small quantities and, to encourage sales, coffee-making demonstrations were held at the back of the shop. Home-made rolls were served with the coffee and thus began the cafes and the bakery.

In 1916 the second shop was opened in Westmoreland Street, which was followed ten years later by the Grafton Street cafe. The latter originally housed the famous Whyte's Academy. Opened in 1758, Samuel Whyte's English grammar school taught many celebrated figures, including Richard Brinsley Sheridan, Thomas Moore, Robert Emmet and the Duke of Wellington. Whyte, who was an active reformist in education, died in 1811.

Though it still appears on the front of the building, the word "Oriental" has been officially dropped since 1972, as Oriental vases and ornaments have not been sold since the second World War. Some special features of the interior are the panelled balcony, the cage-work lift and the stained glass windows executed by Harry Clarke.

The cafe was joint runner-up in the 1983 Corporation Cultural and Environmental Awards.

The Midshipman

This venerable old sailor has kept watch over Murray McGraths in Duke Street for many years now. John Murray, the grand uncle of the present owner found the statue on a quay dump, retrieved it and brought the partly rotting plaster cast to a statue maker for restoration. The statue, a sailor using his sextant, was probably cast as a symbol for the Guild of Ships Chandlers.

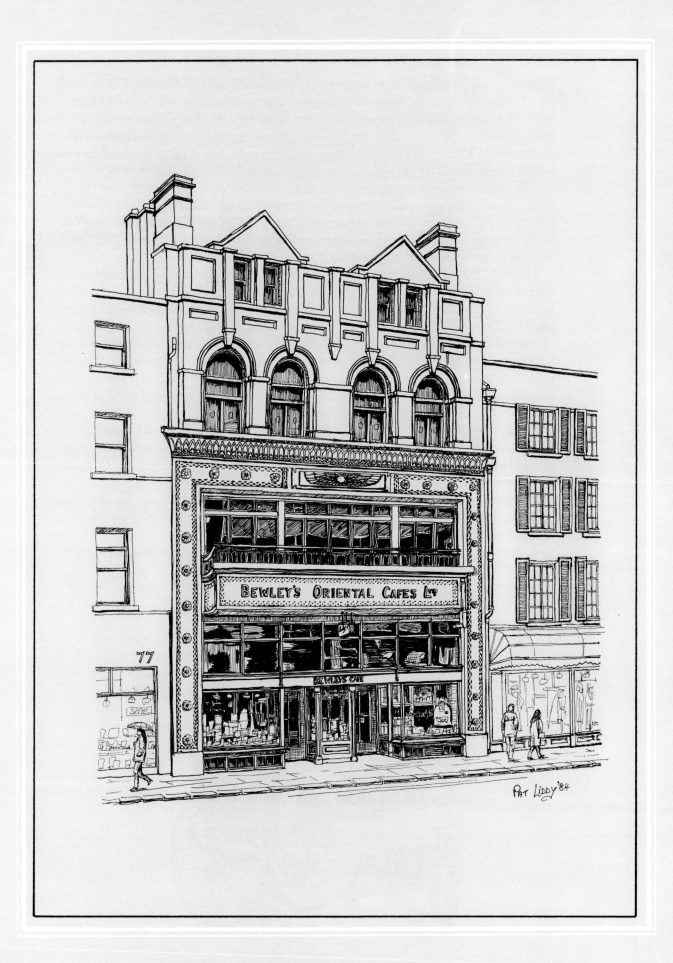

Tobacconists have traded at the corner of Grafton Street and College Green since the German, Augustus Seemuller, started business in 1836 as James Madden. In 1880 the Georgian-style shop was demolished and the Commercial Union Insurance Company erected the present Gothic structure with its familiar turret and gables. James J. Fox, a former employee of Madden's, opened his own tobacco business here in 1881.

The trade has evolved since the days when tobacco was first inhaled through bamboo tubes directly into the nostrils to cause a drug-like euphoria. In time, this habit was followed by the use of long clay pipes, snuff and cigars. Cigarettes only became popular in the last hundred years or so. It seems strange today that doctors once believed that smoking had curative properties.

James J. Fox, a Londoner by birth, had a high reputation as a connoisseur of cigars and this tradition has been faithfully handed down to the present fourth generation. During the second World War, Fox's boasted that they were the only shop in Europe to have a constant supply of Havana cigars.

James's grandson, Fred, can justifiably claim to be the innovator of the world's first duty-free shop at Shannon Airport, following on Seán Lemass's policy for a duty-free zone. He had already been selling cigarettes to the airlines using the recently opened airport when his ideas for a shop were adopted, in a modified form, by the Shannon Airport Authority.

Inside, Fox's possesses the atmosphere one associates with this kind of business. An endless variety of cigar boxes line the shelves and pipes of all shapes and sizes fill the glass cases. The expertise of the staff gladly awaits the enquiring customer, who will be offered a service reminiscent of a bygone age.

Number 36 College Green, next door to Fox's, was occupied by the Ulster Bank in 1862 and later from 1894 to 1973 by Stokes Bros. and Pim, the fore-runners of Stokes, Kennedy and Crowley, chartered accountants. Robert Stokes was largely responsible for the formation of the Irish Institute in 1888.

Northern Bank, College Green

Built by the architect W.G. Murray in 1824 for the Union Bank, this splendid building was purchased a year later by the Hibernian Bank. It was fairly small at this stage, being only four windows wide. Today Dame Street and College Green are resplendent with fine bank and insurance buildings, but in the 1830s and 1840s the companions and neighbours of the Hibernian Bank were mostly Georgian shops and residences.

In 1878, the building was enlarged along College Green and up into Church Lane. The architect was Sir Thomas Drew, noted for his Belfast Cathedral, Gilbeys in O'Connell Street and the Rathmines Town Hall. The final extension into Andrew Street was completed in 1930.

The Corporation had placed a Preservation Order on the structure before the Northern Bank made its purchase in 1979, but the bank was, in any case, very keen to preserve and enhance the building. With the help of Charles Ellison and Associates, the architects, and McLaughlin and Harvey, the main contractors, a programme of refurbishing was planned.

On the outside, the limestone and Portland stone had to be cleaned. The Andrew Street facade had to be remodelled somewhat to permit vehicle access. Damaged decorative features and ironwork had to be replaced.

Some of the most notable achievements were, however, indoors. While much of the interior space had to be redesigned to accommodate a modern banking facility, a decision was made fully to preserve the main banking hall. This is an exceptional Victorian showpiece with a huge vaulted and plastered ceiling and massive mahogany counters. To complement the ceiling there are no hanging lights. Light is provided upwards from concealed sodium bulbs.

We can take encouragement from such spirited restorations, but they are an expensive business. It cost the Northern Bank four million pounds to complete their refurbishing, but they consider every penny spent worthwhile.

The Northern Bank established its first branch office outside what is now known as Northern Ireland in Clones, Co. Monaghan, 144 years ago. By 1870 the bank had moved as far south as Balbriggan.

The move to Dublin came about in 1888 when the private banking firm of Ball and Company, based in Henry Street, sold their assets to the Northern Bank for £22,850. In 1892 an office was opened in Grafton Street, and it was this office that was eventually replaced by the present building in College Green. There are now over 50 branches in the Republic.

P. LIDDY '83

139

City Hall, Cork Hill

The drawing reveals a side of City Hall previously hidden from view by the now demolished buildings on the other side of Exchange Court.

This massive building was erected in Cork Hill between 1769 and 1779. The earliest known structure of any size to stand on the site was the mediaeval church of Sainte Marie del Dam. Dame Street was named after this church. Cork Hill derives its name from Richard Boyle, first Earl of Cork. He demolished the church around 1600 to make way for his own mansion. A generation later, Cromwell turned this house into his Irish headquarters.

Demolishing whole blocks of Dublin is not a recent phenomenon, as in 1768 all the buildings on Cork Hill were levelled and the site acquired by the Merchant Guilds. They then announced a competition for their new Exchange Building. Thomas Cooley, a London architect, won the contract. He also designed Newgate Prison and drew the original plans for the Four Courts. By a twist of fate, Gandon, who had come second in the competition for the Exchange Building, later took over the Four Courts from Cooley.

The Royal Exchange, as it now came to be known, was requisitioned by the authorities during the rising of 1798. It served as a court martial and interrogation centre. The screams of tortured victims were plainly audible in the street outside. Daniel O'Connell, who later became the Lord Mayor of Dublin, made his first public speech there in 1800. During 1916, the building saw action and a number of rebels were killed here.

Today the building is the headquarters of Dublin Corporation. The Council chamber, where the city councillors meet, is the former coffee room of the Merchants' Guild.

Christ Church Cathedral

When an urgent appeal was launched a few years ago to carry out essential reroofing, refitting of the famous peal of 12 bells and other corrective work on one of Dublin's most cherished buildings, the response was tremendous. Over half a million pounds was subscribed, in the main by Dubliners from every social and religious background who knew the special place of Christ Church in the history and life of their city. Already an important centre for ecumenical activity, the cathedral continues to play a highly respected role in the affairs of the local community and the city as a whole.

Christ Church was founded in 1036 by the Norse King, Sitric, and Donat, the first bishop of Dublin. Built originally as a wooden structure on top of the hill which dominated the mediaeval town, the church was replaced in the 1170s by a stone building, much of which survives today. This rebuilding had been carried out under the patronage of the Norman conqueror, Richard de Clare, known as Strongbow, and the Archbishop of Dublin, Lawrence O'Toole.

For the next 700 years the cathedral served as the state church, and the representatives of the Crown swore their oaths of allegiance within its walls. At least four kings came and prayed here, and the Royal Courts of Justice were held in the adjoining monastic buildings until the erection of the Four Courts. In 1542, following the dissolution of the monasteries by King Henry VIII, a Dean and Chapter were substituted for the Prior and Canons.

The cathedral was disestablished in 1871 and lost its state income. It had already sunk into a semi-ruinous condition, with slums encroaching right up against the walls. A Dublin distiller, Henry Roe, donated a quarter of a million pounds and the slums were cleared away, the church was extensively restored. The Synod Hall, which was built to house the Church of Ireland Synod of Bishops and is not part of the cathedral proper, with its unique connecting covered bridge, was constructed at this time.

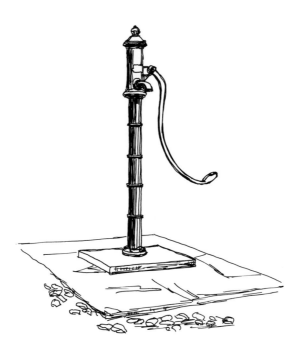

143

The Olympia Theatre, Dame Street

Dan Lowry opened the city's first regular music hall, the Star of Erin, in December 1879. Built over the River Poddle, the hall remained in its original format, with the main entrance in Crampton Court, until 1897. In that year the threatre was reconstructed and the entrance from Dame Street, with its beautiful and characteristic canopy, was added. The old music hall was renamed the Empire Theatre of Varieties. In 1915, Peadar Kearney, the composer of our National Anthem, turned the fire hoses on the orchestra and washed them out of the pit for playing the British Anthem. They never played it in the theatre again.

With the emergence of the Empire, plays, revues and pantomime were added to the original diet of musical variety. In due course the name changed to the Olympia. In 1932, Jimmy O'Dea arrived and stayed until the start of the second World War, at which point he moved to the Gaiety. Albert Barden, the chief usher, fondly remembers the days when there were two nightly performances. The queue for the circle formed around Crampton Court and the patrons who failed to gain admission for the first show were nobly entertained by street singers, dulcimer players, mouth-organists, and jugglers, while they waited for the second performance.

The Olympia suffered a near disaster in 1972 when, during rehearsals for *West Side Story,* part of the building collapsed over the stage. Thankfully, no one was injured. The Corporation and the people of Dublin rallied to the support of the theatre, and after the necessary repairs and some refurbishing were carried out the doors were opened again.

Today, the building remains much the same as it was in 1897. However, with the passage of time and the present shortage of finance, coupled with crippling V.A.T., the furniture and fittings, including the famous front canopy, are in need of urgent attention. In fact, the whole future of this venerable old theatre hangs in the balance. This year the theatre launched a campaign to raise £250,000 to repair and refurbish the building. The scheme includes a comprehensive range of individual and corporate patronage programmes.

145

Foster Place

Foster Place has a unique charm. During the working week, it bustles with commercial activity and with the coming and going of armoured security vans. On Sundays, one can appreciate the dignified grandeur of the ornate balconies and lofty porticos. There are large wrought-iron lantern railings and gates and stylish lamp standards rising from the cobbled street. There are even old granite blocks which once protected the pillars of the present Allied Irish Bank portico from the careless blows of cart wheels.

The cul-de-sac derives its name from John Foster, last Speaker of the Irish Parliament which dissolved itself on 7th June, 1800. The Foster Place portico was a later addition to the main Parliament House, being completed to the designs of James Gandon by Robert Parke in 1797. An underground passage once ran under Foster Place linking the House with Daly's Club, a notorious gambling den frequented by parliamentarians.

After the Act of Union, the Bank of Ireland bought the building for £40,000. They commissioned Francis Johnston, the architect of the G.P.O., to adapt and enlarge the building for their use. He added the curving wall connecting the West portico with the Dame Street facade in 1803 and by 1811 he had completed the annex at the end of Foster Place. This annex was built as an armoury or guardhouse and is crowned by a sculpture called the Kirk Trophy. representing a group of artillery pieces. It was executed by Thomas Kirk, the sculptor of Nelson on the ill-fated Pillar, who was paid a handsome £232-1-0 for his work.

The interior of the bank is reminiscent of a more leisurely age. It boasts a fine ornate style complemented by period writing desks and seats. There is a marble fireplace with an open fire blazing away which is fuelled from an antique coal scuttle. On the nearby wall a roll of honour is dedicated to Irish soldiers who fell at Gallipoli.

The two cannons (one illustrated below) date from the days of the bank militia which was set up to protect the bank in the wake of the 1798 and 1803 insurrections. In other organisations too similar yeomanry were formed to afford protection from seditious rabble and uprisings. A military guard was kept on the bank by the British Army until the Treaty and from then on it became the responsibility of the Irish authorities. The sentry box was used until relatively recently.

E.B.S., Westmoreland Street

The streetscape of Westmoreland Street has altered little since Georgian and Victorian times. The main change has been the recently finished Educational Building Society development.

In the first phase the original Educational chambers at the corner of Fleet Street were refronted by a sheer glass curtain wall. Then in 1975 the E.B.S. acquired the next door premises of *The Irish Times*, The Paradiso Restaurant and Graham's Pharmacy.

The architects, Sam Stephenson and Associates, and the Society planned to preserve the centre piece, the old Paradiso Restaurant, and this they have done. This section, with its terracotta facade, is called the Lafayette Gallery, after the original owners, a famous photographic firm. It was first built in 1912 by the architect George Beckett, an uncle of Samuel Beckett. Its African teak and stained glass windows, vaguely reminiscent of the poop end of a Spanish Galleon, had to be remodelled and replaced. Besides Lafayette's and the Paradiso, this building also housed the honorary consul for Argentina.

To complete phase two the city planners, sensitive to earlier criticisms of the first glass curtain wall, insisted that the other side be spaced by solid panelling of polished granite. This may have been rather unnecessary. In my view the special wavy glass (imported from the U.S.A.) very effectively reflects, in a pleasing crazy-mirror type pattern, the buildings across the street, including the baroque windows of Bewleys.

The scene as you enter the building is totally unexpected. Five floors of stainless steel clad galleries served by a futuristic glass fronted lift, myriads of carnival type light bulbs (over 600 in all) and cascading indoor plants all add up to a very dramatic effect. Maintenance of these bulbs and plants requires, among other measures, the slinging of a safety net between the galleries.

College Street

Last year the front door of number 8 College Street was finally and sadly closed by the Rooney family before the new owners moved in. Thus was ended a tradition of craftsmanship which had been carried on in these premises for over eighty years. John Alexander Rooney founded his firm of engravers in 1843. The first workshop was on Aston Quay, and was moved to College Street at the turn of the century. The firm manufactured steel stamps and utensils, brass plates, memorial brass and, later on, rubber stamps. Another important aspect of their enterprise was the engraving of family crests on silver cutlery, a service very much in demand, at least until after the first World War.

Every afternoon, in their heyday, the workshops fairly bustled with activity as engravers and their apprentices frantically hand-engraved brass memorial plates for the city's undertakers. The orders were usually received only an hour or two before the plates were required. Since most of the engravers tended to work well beyond the normal retiring age it was sometimes the sad duty of a craftsman to dispatch the memorial plate of a deceased colleague who might have worked alongside him only a short time previously.

The shop front, and indeed many of the internal fittings, remained unchanged down through the years. The timber facia is finely carved and includes the customary integrated box for the awning. The front is nicely complemented by the splendid carvings on the outside of the Irish Yeast Company, just two doors away. Until relatively recently families lived above the premises along this block, but regrettably they have for the most part since moved away.

Many readers will have been familiar with the well-fed cats which used to laze in the shop windows of Rooneys. I am glad to report they are alive and well and living in comfort in Dublin 4. I am also happy to say that the new owners have totally refurbished and enhanced the building while maintaining the original style of the shop front.

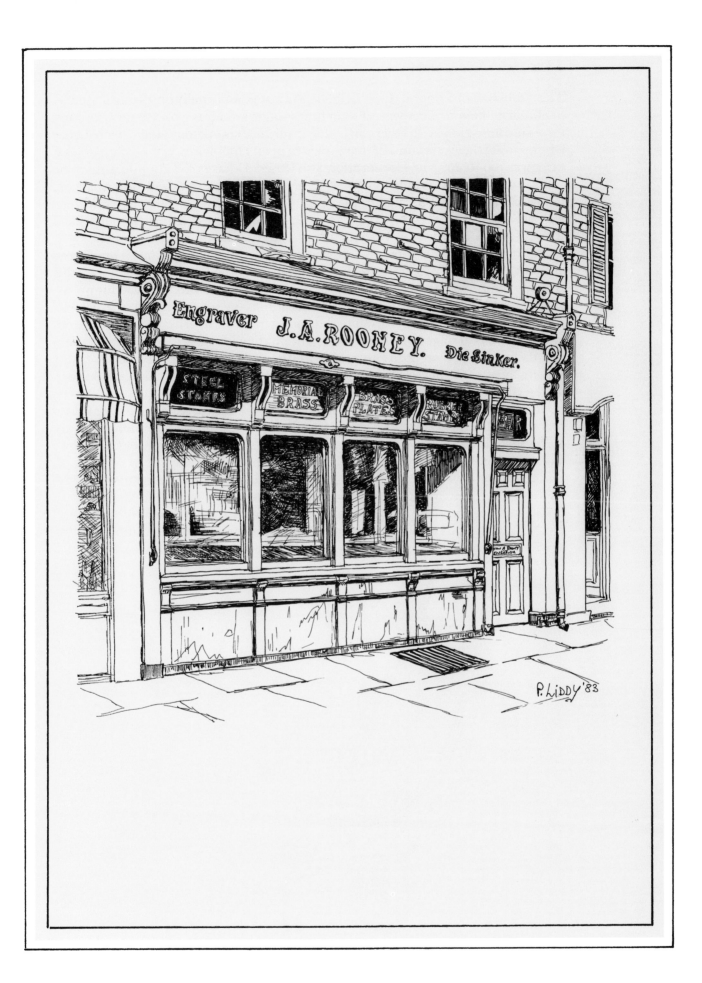

151

Tara Street Fire Station

The Dublin Corporation Fire Brigade Act of 1862 signalled the end of the haphazard, often ineffective and sometimes tragic attempts at fire-fighting by the forces mustered at parish level and by the insurance companies. There were those who opposed the Act, claiming that the extra penny halfpenny in the pound on the rates was too steep. The Corporation also levied a charge for attending fires.

The first station was in Whitehorse Yard, off Winetavern Street, and was soon followed by a second, located in the present Civic Museum. The Headquarters was situated from 1885 in what is now the Irish College of Music in Chatham Row. Chatham Row, inconveniently situated among narrow streets, was replaced on 13th September, 1907 by the new Central Fire Station in Tara Street at a cost of £21,840. Hailed at the time for the many innovations designed by the Brigade Chief and the City Architect, the Station consisted of watching and engine rooms, stables, laundry, workshops and living quarters. When an alarm sounded, the men swished down the slide poles from the overhead dormitories on to the waiting carriages, the horses were automatically released from their stables and took up their own positions and, with the doors opened by a lever over the drivers' heads, the bell-clanging teams swept out in a flurry of hooves galloping on the cobbled streets. Fifty-second "turnouts" were the rule.

The 125 foot high tower was topped by a lookout balcony which was later made redundant when the network of alarm pillars, containing a telephone and an alarm switch, was erected along many of the city's streets. The Tower Clock and its mechanism were modelled exactly on Big Ben.

The Dublin Fire Brigade has grown from a mere handful of men to a force of almost 700 and advanced technology is being increasingly used. The Central Fire Station, so advanced for its day, has now possibly outlived its usefulness. Future roadwidening plans may unfortunately signal the demise of the building and the graceful Florentine-styled tower, which has become a charming part of the Dublin skyline.

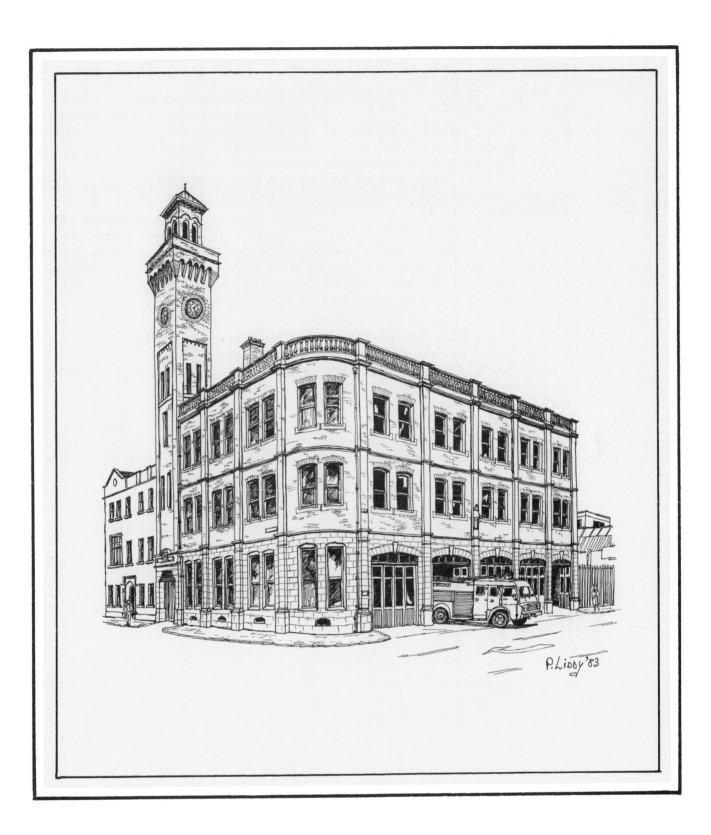

P.Liddy '83

Poolbeg Street

At one time called Shoe Lane, there is little left today of the charm of Poolbeg Street, which once formed an integral part of the warren of narrow cobbled streets and lanes which led from Dublin's 19th century dockland.

An office block now stands at the corner with Hawkins Street where the Theatre Royal was situated until demolished in 1962. This theatre was, in fact, the third in succession to bear the name, the first being built in 1821 on the same site. A night shelter for "Respectable Tramps" was situated behind the Royal until closed down in 1942. It was nicknamed the "Leather Lodgings" because of the cowhide hammocks which were tied to a central rail and whose knots were released every morning to spill out the hapless occupants.

McCairns Motors, which had itself ousted a block of shops and houses, occupied the rest of this side of the street until they moved out to Santry in the early 1950s and were in turn replaced by another office block.

Across the road, the upper end is almost a derelict wasteland with the rear of the gutted Corn Exchange Building clearly visible. The buildings beyond Corn Exchange Place are the only survivors of the old street.

Sam Greer's grandfather started the saddlery and harness business at a time when there were over a hundred men working at this craft in Dublin alone. Today, there are only a handful; Sam's father is probably the only saddler alive in Ireland who plied his trade during the frantic years of the first World War. Now the last horse collar maker in the country, Sam Greer feels that the decline in the trade has been halted with the increasing demand from showdrivers. Bord na gCapall are also sponsoring seven or eight apprentices around the country.

A little further up the street is Mulligan's Bar which was founded in 1782 and still retains all the old atmosphere, from the wooden chairs and tables to the Victorian mirrors and gas lamps. Many a "business" meeting has been held here in the boardroom-like snug.

Memorial on Burgh Quay

On Saturday, 6th May, 1905, a tragedy unfolded in Dublin which received huge media coverage and pushed the grim stories of the Russo-Japanese conflict to one side. About 3.00 p.m. a workman named John Fleming opened a manhole cover at the corner of Hawkins Street and Burgh Quay and descended into the 24-foot deep sewer to investigate a broken pipe. He was almost immediately overcome by deadly sewer gas, as were two of his colleagues who rushed to assist him. A small boy witnessed the scene and sprinted to the policeman standing near O'Connell Bridge.

Constable Patrick Sheahan, aged 29, was a member of the College Street "B" Division of the Dublin Metropolitan Police. A giant of a man, six foot four inches tall and weighing 18 stones, Sheahan was already a legend. Reckless of his own safety, he had once snatched an elderly couple from their collapsing house. On another occasion he had single-handedly stopped a runaway bull in Grafton Street.

Without a second thought, Constable Sheahan climbed into the shaft and hauled out two of the victims before succumbing himself. By this time more volunteers had arrived and for the next hours a grisly circus of would-be rescuers themselves requiring rescue ensued. Eventually, in addition to the deaths of Sheahan and Fleming, twelve other men were taken in agony to Mercer's and Jervis Street hospitals.

The heroism of all concerned, embodied in the death of Sheahan, caused a great wave of emotion across the city. The constable's funeral procession from Mount Argus Church, via Kingsbridge Station, to Glin in Co. Limerick, was attended by thousands of mourners, including hundreds of his police colleagues, city firemen, and Dublin United Tramway workers. Medals for gallantry were presented to 2 firemen and 30 civilians. The Lord Mayor opened an appeal to collect funds for a memorial to honour the memory of Constable Sheahan and the other rescuers. As a result the present monument was erected on Burgh Quay in 1906. It is a pity that the inscription outlining the event is all but worn away. It would be fitting if a co-operative effort by the Corporation and the Garda authorities to restore the monument emerged, especially as it is the only one erected by private citizens in the city, or perhaps in the whole country, as a tribute to a police officer.

P. LIDDY '84

Gas Company, Hawkins Street

Dublin's first gas installation was erected by the Dublin Oil Gaslight Company in 1825 in Brunswick (now Pearse) Street. In 1836 an amalgamation of all existing gas firms established the Alliance Gas Company. A rival enterprise, the Dublin Consumer's Gas Company, was formed by a group of businessmen, led by Daniel O'Connell, in an attempt to improve the reliability and reduce the cost of supply. By 1866 both of these companies were united to become the present Alliance and Dublin Consumers Gas Company.

Cast iron mains – many still exist today – brought gas to all parts of the city and fundamentally improved the lives of the people. Twinkling lights made the street safer at night and hotels, hospitals, businesses and private houses quickly appreciated the benefits of gaslight.

Gas was originally manufactured from coal, and the Company once owned four ships to transport the fuel to Dublin. Later, oil-based naphtha became the feedstock and both the quality and price of gas improved. The oil crisis of 1973 and the subsequent price increases nearly put the Gas Company out of business, but Kinsale Gas may turn around the company's fortunes.

The Company's premises in Hawkins Street were built in the early 1930s. The style was mock Tudor, which was a very fashionable mode in England at the time. The building envelopes an attractive, if dark, laneway. The Tudor windows and archways, wooden balconies and large lanterns would be further enhanced if a little refurbishing was carried out.

The laneway, called Leinster Market, was, in fact, an actual market with secondhand clothes, periwinkle and sweet shops. The Gas Company also had a pay-out hatch in the laneway, but everything was demolished to make way for the present building. A wall plaque dating from the original Dublin Gaslight Company of 1825 was implanted in the wall near the arch entrance to the laneway.

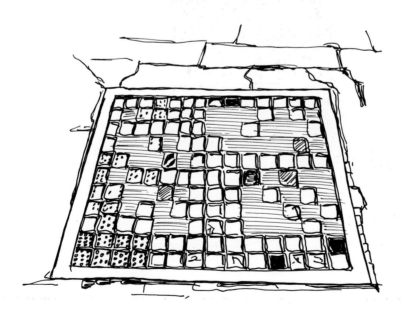

159

D'Olier Street

Two anniversaries which have connections with D'Olier Street were remembered the year *The Irish Times* celebrated its 125th birthday as a daily newspaper. Officially residing at number 13, the newspaper actually occupies a considerable parcel of buildings along D'Olier Street and Fleet Street. Newspaper publishing in the street has not been the sole prerogative of *The Irish Times*. A weekly journal was once published from number 10 and in 1914 Seán MacDiarmada and Tom Clarke moved the offices of *The Irish Freedom* to number 12. The predecessor of the present O'Connell Bridge House, the Carlisle Building, housed the headquarters of Independent Newspapers until they moved to Middle Abbey Street.

On 16th June, 1904, Dignam's funeral in James Joyce's *Ulysses* passed by the premises of Blazes Boylan described as number 15. Just across the street was the Red Bank Restaurant, famous for its oysters, and since converted into a church for the Blessed Sacrament Fathers.

Much of the river end of the street has been altered since it was first conceived by the Wide Street Commissioners in 1802 and the unique uniformity of the elevations has been lost. D'Olier House replaces the demolished premises of T. & C. Martin formerly the Junior Army and Navy Stores. The art deco style of the Gas Company dates from the 1930s. The Regent Hotel has been replaced by the offices of the Irish Civil Service Building Society, who have retained the fine Gothic corner building dating from 1894, though it is somewhat spoiled by neon advertising.

At the other end of the street, grandly occupying Hewett's Corner, is a striking edifice. It was lavishly constructed in the 1890s as the prestigious Southern Ireland branch office for the tobacco manufacturers Gallaher and Company. The splendid wooden counters and fittings of the original ground floor tobacco retail outlet are still in situ. The rest of the building was erected as an office block and, in 1900, 20 solicitors and insurance brokers practised from here.

D'Olier Street was named after Jeremiah D'Olier, a Huguenot and one-time Sheriff of Dublin.

After its removal from the old offices of *The Irish Times* in Westmoreland Street, the famous clock languished for many years in oblivion. Magnificently restored, this elegant timepiece was re-erected recently in D'Olier Street.

160

The Zoological Gardens

Since the 1960s the Tudor-styled thatched gatehouse, so much the symbol of the Zoo, has no longer been used. This charming building was built about 1832, two years after the inauguration of the Zoological Society of Dublin. The current annual upkeep, including the regular rethatching, of the gatehouse is sponsored by the Educational Building Society. The land on which the Zoological Gardens now stand was granted to the Society by the Lord Lieutenant, the Duke of Northumberland, in 1830. Unfortunately, he actually did not have any authority to grant title on what was the King's land, and to this day the Society only holds the property by licence. Queen Victoria became patroness in 1838, and the society changed its name to the Royal Zoological Society of Ireland. The Zoo gained an international reputation for the breeding of lions, one of which for many years introduced all MGM films.

Primrose Cottage, Blackhorse Avenue

Once a narrow winding country road skirting the northern end of the Phoenix Park, Blackhorse Avenue is now being widened to accommodate the locality's burgeoning housing and apartment developments. Standing defiant against the metamorphosis occurring all around it is one of the city's last surviving thatched cottages. Formerly flanked by extensive commercial orchards, the almost 300-year old Primrose Cottage was beautifully set off by an attractive garden. Road expansion has since filched most of the front garden space, and the orchards have been replaced by blocks of flats. The whole area, including Blind Lane (now Nephin Road) was popular for market gardening and was well served by natural wells. One such supply, Poor Man's Well, still exists today and is situated between the cottage and the Cabra Gate entrance to the Phoenix Park.

The nearly two foot thick walls are not made of stone as might be expected, but from a mixture of clay and straw. The small windows date from the time when larger openings attracted higher taxes. The owners of the cottage can testify that the thick walls and thatched roof genuinely keep the house warm in winter and cool in summer.

Gardín na n'Anamhithe.

P. Liddy '83

The Casino, Marino

Every day thousands of motorists driving through the Malahide Road-Griffith Avenue junction pass a classical building set in a field next to the splendour of the O'Brien Institute. It may seem insignificant and unremarkable from the road but it is internationally renowned, being considered one of the finest examples of Palladian architecture in the world.

Because of its scale and massive ornamentation it appears small until you stand beside it and realise that it is the size of a three storey house.

For instance, there are five flights of stairs and fifty-four steps from the ground to the roof level. There is also a huge basement area with dungeon-like storage rooms set into the outside retaining wall. In all there are sixteen rooms.

It was designed for the Earl of Charlemont by William Chambers (who designed Charlemont House, now the Municipal Art Gallery) and built by the Italian mason, Simon Vierpyl, between 1765 and 1771 at a cost of £60,000. The sculptor of the ornaments, Edward Smyth, was the same man who executed the Statue of Commerce on top of the Custom House dome.

The building is very cleverly designed. The roof urns serve as chimneys, the four outer Truscan columns are hollowed to act as drainpipes and the rooms have a central heating system built into the walls and served from the fireplaces.

P. Liddy '82

Swiss Cottage, Santry

The recently opened by-pass will remove the necessity for traffic to trundle through Santry on the way to and from Dublin Airport and the cities and towns further north. The village can now return to a relative obscurity. However, it is a radically changed community from that of even 40 years ago and has probably suffered more in the name of progress than virtually any other of the villages which have been swallowed up in the expanding city.

Erected in 1702 and burnt to a shell in the 1940s, Santry Court was the huge mansion home of the Barrys, the Barons of Santry. Morton Stadium and the adjoining car park are situated on the grounds of this mansion. The Protestant Church of St Pappin, built in 1709, and housing an important collection of Irish brass, still stands, but gone is the old village forge with its door fashioned in the shape of a horseshoe. Gone too are ten of the eleven Swiss-style cottages built as a model village by Lady Domville of Santry Court in 1840. She had just returned from a holiday in Switzerland, where she had got the romantic notion for her scheme. Designing houses in the Swiss idiom had become fashionable in Ireland and England, most likely as a result of the gentry visting the new resorts in the Alps.

Sometime ago I saw to my alarm that the cottage was being dismantled. However, this was part of the plan to incorporate the building into a new office block which was constructed around the original cottage in similar style. This unusual and welcome development was the brainchild of John R. Moore Construction Ltd. and was completed in June 1984.

P. LIDDY '83

167

Corballis House, Dublin Airport

Many visitors to Dublin Airport must wonder at the pleasant incongruity of a Georgian country mansion cheekily squatting in front of the modern terminal building.

The history of Corballis house is known to date back beyond the beginning of the 18th century. In the early 1700s it was acquired by the then Lord Mayor of Dublin, Thomas Wilkinson. He passed it on to his son, who in turn granted it to his son, Sir Henry Wilkinson, the Recorder of Kilkenny. *The Freeman's Journal* of August, 1809 makes reference to a banquet being held there. The name Corballis may be derived from Cor Bhaile, "odd town", though this is not certain.

The house represents very early Georgian house design and internally, except for minor alterations, it remains much as it was in its early days. The floor of the entrance hall is beautifully tiled and recent refurbishing revealed hand-made nails which may have been produced by the local smithy. The "ivy" growing around much of the outside walls is not ivy at all but a cultivated vine which was capable at one time of bearing grapes.

Corballis House has been used by Aer Lingus as a training centre since 1954, and airport staff tell stories ranging from rumours of a resident ghost to the early days when they fed the many pheasants in the field next to the house. Badgers, rabbits and the odd fox were also to be seen.

Those days are gone for ever, alas, but thanks to the conservation-minded Airport Authority, Aer Rianta, and to its tenants, Aer Lingus, the future of this fine old country house seems assured.

As illustrated below other Georgian Houses have not fared so well!

List of Main Illustrations

For further reading

There is simply a huge collection of books written about Dublin so I will only attempt to list a selection of my favourites:

Guide to Historic Dublin Adrian MacLoughlin, Gill & Macmillan Ltd., Dublin, 1979.

Dublin Peter Somerville-Large, Granada Publishing Ltd., London, 1979.

Dublin 1660-1860 Maurice Craig, Allen Figgis & Co. Ltd., Dublin, 1980.

Dublin Desmond Clarke, B.T. Batsford Ltd., London, 1977.

Lost Dublin Frederick O'Dwyer, Gill & Macmillan Ltd., Dublin, 1977.

Me Jewel and Darlin' Dublin Éamonn MacThomáis, The O'Brien Press, Dublin, 1980.

James Joyce's Odyssey Frank Delaney, Hodder and Stoughton Ltd., London, 1982.

The Liberties of Dublin Edited by Elgy Gillespie, The O'Brien Press Ltd., Dublin, 1973.